Magico-Religious Groups and Ritualistic Activities

A Guide for First Responders

Tony M. Kail

CRC Press
Taylor & Francis Group
Boca Raton London New York

CRC Press is an imprint of the
Taylor & Francis Group, an **informa** business

CRC Press
Taylor & Francis Group
6000 Broken Sound Parkway NW, Suite 300
Boca Raton, FL 33487-2742

International Standard Book Number-13: 978-1-4200-5186-5 (Hardcover)

Library of Congress Cataloging-in-Publication Data

Kail, Tony M.
Magico-religious groups and ritualistic activities : a guide for first responders / Tony M. Kail.
p. cm.
Includes bibliographical references and index.
ISBN 978-1-4200-5186-5 (alk. paper)
1. Magic--Religious aspects. 2. Religion and culture. I. Title.

BL65.M2K35 2008
203--dc22 2007033001

Visit the Taylor & Francis Web site at
http://www.taylorandfrancis.com

and the CRC Press Web site at
http://www.crcpress.com

Contents

Preface xv
Acknowledgments xvii
Author xix

1 Introduction 1

First Responders 1
View from the Patient's Perspective 1
Risks for First Responders 2
Solutions 3
References 4

2 An Introduction to Religious Culture for Responders 7

Cultural Competency 7
Anthropological Terms 9
Magico-Religious Cultures 10
References 11

3 Neopaganism 13

Beliefs and Practices 13
  Neopaganism 14
History of Wicca 15
  Traditions 16
    Alexandrian Wicca 16
    British Traditional Wicca 16
    Celtic Wicca 16
    Dianic Wicca 16
    Eclectic Wicca 16
    Gardenarian Wicca 16
    Georgian Wicca 17
    Hereditary Wicca 17
    Mohsian Tradition 17
    Strega Tradition 17

Beliefs	17
Deities of Wicca	18
Ethics	18
Group Structure	19
Ritual Tools	20
Rituals and Ceremonies	21
Correspondences	21
Preparation of Ritual Area	22
Consecration of Ritual Tools and Implements	22
Grounding	22
Casting the Circle	22
Calling the Quarters	23
Invocation of Deity	23
Energy Is Raised	24
Spellwork	24
Cakes/Wine	24
Opening and Banishment of the Circle	24
Rites of Passage	24
Holy Days	25
Samhain	25
Yule	25
Imbolc	25
Ostara	26
Beltane	26
Litha	26
Lammas	26
Mabon	26
Sacred Spaces	26
Health and Sickness	29
Cord Healing	29
Aromatherapy	29
Chanting	29
Auric Healing	29
Chakras	31
Absent Healing	31
Herbalism	31
Ritual Body Art	33
Smudging	34
Candles	34
Destruction of Illness	35
Articles of Comfort	36
Source of Sickness	37
Taboos	37

Responder Issues 38
Weapons/Harmful Implements 39
References 39

4 Santeria (Regla de Ocha) 41

History of Santeria 41
Beliefs and Practices 43
The Deities of Santeria 43
Elegua 43
Ogun 45
Ochosi 45
Oshun 45
Obatala 45
Chango 45
Oya 45
Yemaya 46
Babalu-Aye 46
Olokun 46
Orula/Orunmila 47
Osain 47
The Ibejis 47
Aganyu 47
Inle 48
Oko 48
The Ancestors 48
Group Structure 49
Rituals and Ceremonies 50
Receiving the Necklaces 50
Warriors 52
Cofa 52
Kariocha 53
Obi 54
Diloggun 56
Patakis 56
Offerings and Sacrifices 56
Addimu 56
Ebbo 57
Trance Possession 58
Espiritismo 59
Brujeria 60
Holy Days 61
Itutu 62

Sacred Spaces 62
Healing and Sickness 62
Methods of Healing 63
Santeria Herbalism 64
Mercury 66
Articles of Comfort 66
Idé 66
Macuto 66
Responder Issues 67
References 69

5 Palo and Kongo Religions 71

Bantu Traditions 71
Bantu Religious Elements 72
Beliefs and Practices 73
Nganga: The Cauldron 75
Bones 75
Sacred Spaces 76
Lucero 78
Siete Rayos 78
Zarabanda 78
Mama Sholan 78
Centelle Ndoki 79
Tiembla Tierra 79
Madre de Agua 80
Francisco and Francisca 80
Seven Congos 80
Group Structure 80
Rituals and Ceremonies 81
Divination 81
Sacrifices 81
Initiation 82
Herbalism 84
Articles of Comfort 85
Healing and Sickness 86
Responder Issues 86
References 87

6 Voodoo 89

Beliefs and Practices 89
Rada 90
Legba 90

Marasa 90
Loko 91
Ayizan 91
Sobo 92
Agassou 92
La Sirene 92
Azaka 92
Damballah Wedo 92
Ayida Wedo 92
Ezili Freda 92
Ogou Group 93
Agwe 93
Petro 93
Simbi 93
Kalfu (Carrefour) 93
Gran Bwa 93
Ezili Danto (Erzulie Dantor) 94
Marinette-Bwa-Chech 94
Ti-Jean Petro 94
Simbi 94
Gede 94
Baron Samedi 94
Maman Brigette 95
Spiritual Bodies and Guardians 95
Group Structure 95
Ritual Tools 96
Asson 96
Bottle 97
Chromolithograph 97
Flags 97
Govi 97
Packets 98
Swords 98
Ogan 98
The Triangle 98
Conch Shell 98
Zins 98
Drums 98
Ceremonies 99
Entrance 100
The Priye Ginen 100
Manje Loa: The Sacrifice 100
Rites of Passage 101

Spirit Possession 101
Initiation 102
Marriage 102
Zombies 102
Sacred Days 102
Sacred Spaces 103
Health and Sickness 105
Other Traditions of Voodoo 106
Dominican Voodoo (21 Divisiones) 106
Dahomean or West African Voodoo 106
New Orleans Voodoo 106
Responder Issues 107
References 108

7 Curanderismo 109

Beliefs and Practices 109
Our Lady of Guadalupe 110
San Martin de Porres 111
San Martin Caballero 111
Judas Tudeo 112
Santa Marta 113
San Simon 113
Jesus Malverde 113
Juan Soldado 113
Dr. Jose Gregorio Hernandez 113
San Toribio Romo 113
Santa Muerte 114
Other Folk Saints 114
Group Structure 115
Healing and Sickness 117
Methods of Healing 118
Herbalism 119
Objects of Healing 120
Horseshoe Amulet 120
Lodestone 121
Scapulario 121
Milagro 121
La Manito de Coral 121
Ojo de Venado 121
Responder Issues 122
Reference 124

8 Closing Issues **125**

Behavior 125
Language 125
Patience 125
Communication 125
References 126

Glossary of Cultural Terms **127**

Index of Symbols **133**

Subject Index **139**

List of Figures

Figure 1.1	The growing number of magico-religious practitioners in society creates new challenges for responders hoping to attain cultural competency.	3
Figure 1.2	Cultural competency can assist responders in avoiding violation of cultural taboos, such as the handling of religious artifacts considered "sacred."	4
Figure 2.1	Identifying "family resemblances" or common concepts among religious cultures can assist responders in strategies related to communication and approach.	8
Figure 2.2	The magical Law of Contact at work.	11
Figure 3.1	Responders may observe images of female deities from a number of world religions used to represent the Goddess of the Wiccan religion.	15
Figure 3.2	A High Priestess places a cord around the initiate.	19
Figure 3.3	A Wiccan altar.	27
Figure 3.4	Upon entering a residence, responders may discover cultural objects related to a patient's faith as decorations.	28
Figure 3.5	Figures representing the God and Goddess of Wicca.	28
Figure 3.6	A ritual healing is being performed to remove negative energies that are causing problems in the life of the patient.	30
Figure 3.7	Candle magic is practiced in many different world religions.	35
Figure 3.8	Responders may discover tattoos and ritual body art on patients.	36
Figure 3.9	Responders may encounter rituals performed in outdoor settings.	37
Figure 3.10	Responders should avoid touching shrines and altars.	38
Figure 4.1	Shown are various ritual artifacts representing the deities of the Santeria religion.	44
Figure 4.2	A shrine to the Orisha Elegua.	44
Figure 4.3	A statue known as Chango Macho is used in spiritual workings.	46
Figure 4.4	The soperas of Yemaya and Oshun.	47
Figure 4.5	Respect for dead ancestors is a concept found in many African traditional religions.	49
Figure 4.6	A Santero wearing the traditional white clothing and Elekes of the Santeria faith.	51
Figure 4.7	The Sopera contains the "secrets" of the Orishas.	54

Figure 4.8 The Orishas speak to practitioners through the coconut shells known as the Obi. 55
Figure 4.9 The coconut shells (Obi) are "thrown" after the Orisha is given three drops of water. 56
Figure 4.10 An example of offerings to the Orishas. 57
Figure 4.11 A priestess conducts a ceremony for the Orishas. 67
Figure 4.12 Responders should use caution if handling ritual objects during an investigation. 68
Figure 5.1 The Nganga is the central vessel used in Palo Mayombe and other assorted Kongo faiths. 72
Figure 5.2 Human bones are components that are traditionally used in the Nganga to represent the Nfumbe or spirits of the dead. 73
Figure 5.3 The cana brava is a piece of cane or bamboo that is filled with mercury and sealed off. 76
Figure 5.4 The working space of a Palero is shown. 77
Figure 5.5 The Firma is a drawing that represents Bantu religious concepts, such as deities, rituals and the intention of practices. 78
Figure 5.6 Responders may discover the presence of blood and remains of animals in the shrines of Palo practitioners. 79
Figure 5.7 Francisco is a figure that represents deified African ancestors and is also used in shrines to represent the Mupungu Siete Rayos. 80
Figure 5.8 The Chamalongos are used as a divination tool to communicate with the spirits inside the Nganga. 82
Figure 5.9 This Nganga was discovered near the scene of a double homicide. 83
Figure 5.10 The initiate stands on this firma to make the Pacto or "pact" with the dead (Nfumbe). 84
Figure 5.11 Shown are bottles of the substance Chamba, which is a liquid that is sprayed onto ritual vessels. 85
Figure 5.12 Responders should be aware that the use of mercury in a ritualistic vessel is quite common in Palo Mayombe. 87
Figure 6.1 This celebratory shrine contains many objects representing the deities of Haitian Voodoo. 91
Figure 6.2 The priest (Houngan) and the priestess (Mambo) perform sacred baths using herbs and water. 96
Figure 6.3 The priestess, known as the Mambo, takes the rattle called an Asson. 97
Figure 6.4 The three-legged pot known as the Zin is filled with oil and burnt as a lamp. 99
Figure 6.5 A mural of a traditional Voodoo ceremony. 100
Figure 6.6 An altar dedicated to those lost in the tragedy of Hurricane Katrina. 107
Figure 7.1 An altar dedicated to the folk saints of Curanderismo. 110

Figure 7.2	An altar dedicated to Our Lady of Guadalupe.	111
Figure 7.3	Responders may encounter statues of folk saints and offerings to the spirits that they represent.	112
Figure 7.4	Folk saints, such as San Martin Caballero, bring good fortune to those who honor him in their homes and businesses.	112
Figure 7.5	Santa Muerte is a folk saint who is reported to be honored as the patron saint of criminals.	114
Figure 7.6	Amulets and talismans are sold by the Curandero/Curandera to provide health and healing.	116
Figure 7.7	Herbs may be prescribed by a Yerbero who serves as an herbal specialist to the Hispanic community.	116
Figure 7.8	Patients may use herbal soaps and oils designed to physically and spiritually heal aches and pains.	119
Figure 7.9	Patients may wear necklaces dedicated to folk saints.	
Figure 7.10	The Ojo De Vando or Deer's Eye is used to ward off the evil eye or Mal de Ojo.	121
Figure 7.11	An amulet used to ward off the evil eye.	122
Figure 7.12	The Curandero is the local healer, psychiatrist and priest.	123

Preface

Magico-Religious Groups and Ritualistic Activities: A Guide for First Responders was written to give responders a cultural bridge of understanding when interacting with the various magico-religious cultures of the world. The cultural intricacies that exist in religion present a challenge to the believers of these faiths and to the outsiders who encounter them. Artifacts, rituals and symbols are but small pieces of religious culture; these aspects can be seen with the naked eye by both believer and nonbeliever. The meanings attached to these aspects are hidden somewhere in the mythology of religious culture.

Understanding the hidden meanings behind these artifacts affects how responders choose to interact with patients who belong to these religious cultures. Knowledge of cultural taboos can give responders an advantage in communicating with a patient. Understanding that physical illness can have a "magical" significance can help responders in interpreting patient behavior.

There are several aspects of religious culture that can be understood through the disciplines of cultural anthropology and religious studies. This book seeks to draw from these disciplines and place religious culture in a context that will be relevant to the first responder. The complexities of each of these religious cultures cannot be limited to one chapter, but this book provides an elementary understanding of the basic concepts of these cultures.

Chapter 1 provides an important introduction to the need for transcultural communication skills and cultural competency for responders. Chapter 2 introduces readers to the concept of magic in religious culture and the common elements found in this culture. Chapter 3 (Neopaganism) provides responders with information on the culture of contemporary witchcraft and the various indigenous religions that are being revitalized in Western society. Chapter 4 (Santeria [Regla de Ocha]) is an examination of the Afro-Caribbean religion of the Yoruba people. Issues relating to sacred objects, biohazards and cultural taboos are a special focus. Chapter 5 (Palo and Kongo Religions) looks into the culture of Palo Mayombe and the various Bantu faiths. Chapter 6 (Voodoo) introduces the reader to the practices and beliefs of this Haitian-based religion. The actual culture of the Voudon faith is presented to help responders separate "fact" from "fantasy." Chapter 7 (Curanderismo) looks at the phenomena of folk saints and folk healing among members of the Latin community. Herbal healing is examined as a practice that is widely used among the healers and patients in the community. Chapter 8 (Closing Issues) assesses cultural aspects using *Kleinman's Tool to Elicit Health Beliefs in Clinical Encounters.* The Appendix (Index of Symbols) contains a catalog of symbols used in the artifacts and practices of magico-religious groups. And, finally, a Glossary of Cultural Terms provides readers with a lexicon of cultural terms that patients from various cultures may use when communicating with responders.

Public service agencies should provide employees with the tools necessary to properly assess situations and to effectively communicate with the growing population of magico-religious groups. Cultural competency can ensure cultural diversity and protection of deeply held religious faiths. It can also protect the health of responders and protect society from dangerous practices. Cultural competency does not mean that we condone or disapprove of a culture; it simply means that we understand each other's worldview. It is my hope that this book serves as a map to those unfamiliar cultures that responders may encounter.

Tony Kail

Forensic Theology Consultants

Acknowledgments

There are a number of people who have helped me understand the world of magico-religious culture. It was through the numerous introductions and relationships with members of these spiritual communities that I have been allowed to photograph and document the altars and shrines of believers. It is through the courtesy and hospitality of these practitioners that I have been permitted to witness ceremonies and rites of passage among various groups. Thank you for sharing your culture for the greater benefit of understanding.

I am deeply grateful to those who are involved in the pursuit of public safety. From law enforcement to emergency medical services (EMS), your service to our society is invaluable. I am grateful to those of you who have helped me understand the needs and demands of first responders.

Finally, it is only with the support of my faith, family and friends that I am able to continue this work. You are my rock.

Acknowledgments

[illegible]

Author

Tony Kail is the founder of and serves as director of the Forensic Theology Resource Center at Jackson, Tennessee. He has served as a consultant and lecturer to numerous regional, state and federal law enforcement agencies on the subject of magico-religious groups and has 17 years of experience in research and fieldwork with these groups. Kail also has served as a deputy sheriff and as an animal cruelty investigator for the Madison County Humane Society.

He has worked on a number of ethnographic research projects with members of the Neopagan and African religious communities. His research has been used to train police and forensic and public safety agencies around the world. Kail has conducted research in East Africa among members of African traditional religious groups, and has observed and documented hundreds of hours of rituals and ceremonies among magico-religious groups in the United States and abroad.

Kail has served as an adjunct instructor in the Police Sciences Division of Nashville State Community College and Jackson State Community College (Tennessee). His unique approach to magico-religious groups and ritualistic activities is presented in the R.U.L.E.S. (Ritualistic Understanding for Law Enforcement Strategies) program, which he developed. He combines his knowledge of cultural and forensic anthropology with law enforcement strategies to provide agencies with effective tools in approaching religious cultures.

He has authored several publications on magico-religious culture, ritualistic crime and transcultural communication, and has begun work on collecting and documenting ritual tools and artifacts used in magico-religious practices throughout the world. The collection currently contains over 500 pieces and will serve as a research resource for cultural and physical anthropologists, law enforcement and forensic investigators.

Kail is a member of the International Association of Counterterrorism and Security Professionals, the Tennessee chapter of the International Association of Identification and the Public Safety Writers of America Association.

Author

Introduction 1

First Responders

First responders can come from a variety of disciplines, such as fire service responders or police officers, or one may work in emergency medical services (EMS) or volunteer his/her time in a rescue service. Regardless of your background, the challenges that you encounter when meeting people on emergency calls are that they are typically in a very fragile state. The sound of a siren or the appearance of a uniform may be the only thing that brings a victim of violence or illness comfort when in a state of trauma. It is in these times that you serve as protector, healer and counselor to those in need of your assistance.

In order for responders to effectively provide quality care, it is necessary for service personnel to keep themselves protected and safe. This means assessing scenes for any overt hazards as well as knowing how to detect the subtle, not so obvious dangers.

As you encounter patients from a variety of backgrounds, you discover that race, religion and economic status take the back seat when providing care. However, there are situations in which elements of a religious culture can present unique obstacles to providing proper treatment. What happens when the elements of one's faith become issues that may harm his/her health or confuse those providing emergency care?

What if in the course of "assessing the scene" you encounter a patient in the middle of a religious ceremony that includes some things that make you personally uncomfortable. Candles, knives or even blood at a scene can create an element of fear and apprehension in us all. A patient who is wearing a hooded robe or jewelry with strange symbols could appear menacing to an outsider. How would this affect you?

View from the Patient's Perspective

Imagine yourself as a member of an immigrant Haitian family that has recently moved into the U.S. Midwest. In addition to the language and cultural barriers that present everyday challenges to your family, your religious faith is kept secret from local residents. Voodoo: Just the mention of that word makes most Westerners uneasy. Books and movies talk about your religion as some sort of demon worship that practices human sacrifice. But, you as a Haitian grew up knowing the gods and goddesses of Haitian Voodoo as spirits of nature that your family openly served for several generations. Your experience with Voodoo has been something very different from that depicted in the media. Now, imagine that your mother has become very ill. She clutches her chest experiencing severe pain. You dial 911 for help. As responders arrive at your home, they can plainly see the altars and shrines that are set up around the house. One responder's eye catches the skull on your altar that represents the Ghede family of spirits.

You can relate to the feeling of fear on the responders' faces. As they take your mother's hand, you notice that she is wearing her beaded bracelet that gives her spiritual protection. You hope that they don't remove it.

As a responder, it is necessary to place yourself in the role of the patient. It is there that you begin to not only understand the patient's healthcare needs, but also the need for physical and verbal communication that will bring them peace and allow them to openly communicate.

Risks for First Responders

Aside from the potential threats that exist in these types of scenes, there are several unique risks that may be present. While responding to a call involving a patient experiencing heart problems, a scene involving the Santeria religion may also contain additional risks to patient and responder. Mercury may be present at the scene, as it is used in rituals and in amulets. Flammable liquids, such as the cologne "Florida Water," may be present near heat sources. It is in these situations that it is important for the responder to know what possible dangers might be present alongside cultural elements (Figure 1.1).

Nonlaw enforcement personnel responding to scenes may encounter elements that make it necessary to call authorities to assist at the scene. A responder encountering practitioners of Palo Mayombe may observe the sacred vessel known as the "Nganga" at the scene. The human bones that are used in the making of the religious shrine may be present and in violation of state health regulations.

Finally, as you interact with your patient, you may find that the patient is describing pains that he or she attributes to spiritual matters. The pains may also have unfamiliar folk names, such as Susto or Empacho. The Diagnostic and Statistcal Manual of Mental Disorders–IV (DSM-IV) manual, which is used to diagnose mental disorders, includes a section on the phenomenon of "cultural bound syndromes."[1] These are illnesses caused by a cultural belief.

Figure 1.1 The growing number of magico-religious practitioners in society creates new challenges for responders hoping to attain cultural competency.

One example is the cultural concept of Rootwork, which is a collective term used to describe the use of roots and herbs in spells and magical rituals. Rootwork is practiced in many religious cultures, but is known primarily as a term used in the Southern United States by practitioners of Hoodoo or Southern folk magic. The symptoms that result from the cultural acceptance of rootwork as a form of aggravation include anxiety, nausea, vomiting, diarrhea, weakness, dizziness, fear of poisoning and fear of death. Responders may encounter patients that show these symptoms and who disclose a belief in Rootwork.

You may find that patients of various cultures utilize healing methods that appear unusual. Environmental control is the ability of members of a culture to plan activities that control nature or direct environmental factors. This includes systems of traditional health and illness beliefs, the practice of folk medicine, and the use of traditional healers. This influences the way in which the members of a culture define health and illness and how they might seek treatment.[2]

Solutions

These situations create unique challenges for first responders. However, there are a number of solutions that can assist the responder in providing quality healthcare, respect for diversity and remaining safe from hazards at the scene.

Figure 1.2 Cultural competency can assist responders in avoiding violation of cultural taboos, such as the handling of religious artifacts considered "sacred."

The field of healthcare has incorporated a number of strategies in dealing with members of various cultures they may encounter. Some agencies, like the Boston Healing Landscape Project[3] in Boston, Massachusetts, have trained healthcare professionals with classes covering subjects, such as African Diaspora religions and the use of herbs in the Haitian community.

Some agencies have incorporated networking with ritual specialists from the various religious communities. These specialists, known as "cultural brokers," assist medical professionals by providing spiritual services alongside traditional Western healthcare. The office of cultural brokers was first discovered when anthropologists observed that certain people in some societies could act as middlemen and bring understanding between colonial governments and world cultures.[4]

It is safe to assume that not every agency has the means or staffing to develop programs such as these. As a first responder, you can develop a degree of "cultural competency" that will allow you to operate in the realms of various cultures. Cultural competency provides us with a strategy to accomplish the goals of proper response and assistance to patients without being sidetracked by cultural shock. An informed plan of action will give us the tools necessary to communicate successfully and lessen the possibility of alienating the patient (Figure 1.2).

References

1. American Psychiatric Association (1994). *Diagnostic and Statistical Manual of Mental Disorders DSM-IV* (4th ed.). APPI: Arlington, VA.

2. Spector, Rachel E. (2003). *Cultural Diversity in Health and Illness.* Prentice Hall: Upper Saddle River, NJ.
3. Boston Healing Landscape Project (2007). http://www.bmc.org/pediatrics/special/bhlp
4. National Center for Cultural Competence (2004). *Bridging the Cultural Divide in Health Care Settings: The Essential Role of Cultural Broker Programs.* http://www11.georgetown.edu/research/gucchd/nccc/documents/Cultural_Broker_Guide_English.pdf

An Introduction to Religious Culture for Responders

2

Cultural Competency

When a responder encounters a culture that he or she is unfamiliar with, there is a concept known as cultural competency that would benefit the responder in assessing the patient and the scene. Cultural competency has been defined as "a set of values and principles, and demonstrative behaviors, attitudes, policies and structures that enable organizations to operate cross-culturally."[1] In looking at various religious cultures, we can begin to form a plan of cultural competency by looking at some of the concepts of cultural anthropology as a guideline to understanding culture.

Cultural anthropology utilizes a number of techniques and theories in which man can look at other cultures and find commonalities in concepts. Perhaps you have a Judeo-Christian background. Encountering members of the Wiccan faith, you can see some common concepts that are familiar to your belief system. The use of prayer, sacred space and even communion can be seen in both belief systems. These commonalities make it easy for you to understand the other cultures around you (Figure 2.1).

One writer has penned the term *family resemblances* as a way to describe the common elements found in religious cultures.[2] These family resemblances can be seen in the religions that we will be discussing in this book.

Some of the common elements that we see in religious culture include:

Belief in Supernatural or Superior Beings: Supernatural beings may be referred to as gods, angels, demons, spirits or as cultural-specific names such as the deities of Santeria, known as Orisha; the spirits of Voodoo, known as Loa or the elemental spirits in Wicca, known as Watchers.

The Significance of Human Life: Religion gives meaning to life. Each person is created for a reason that is dictated by the religious culture. For instance, the religion of Santeria teaches that man is born to serve the Orishas (deities) and that each person has a guardian Orisha.

A Moral Code: Religious beliefs surrounding a moral code seek to give guidelines for personal ethics. The religion of Wicca observes a moral code known as the Wiccan Rede.

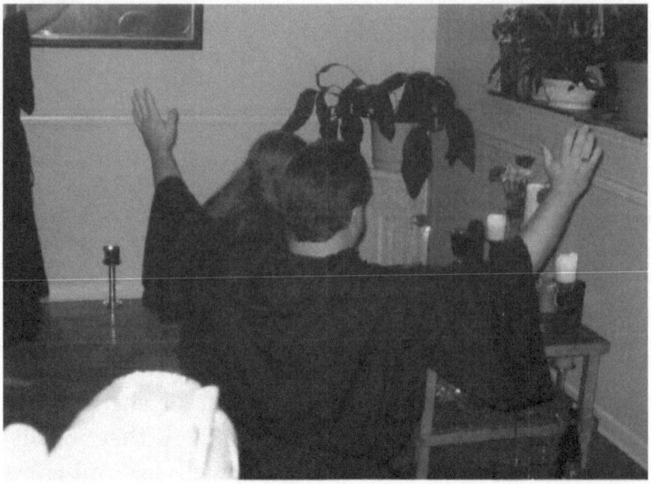

Figure 2.1 Identifying "family resemblances" or common concepts among religious cultures can assist responders in strategies related to communication and approach.

An Account of Evil: Most religions have a form of evil or opposition. In a patient's view, evil may be the cause of sickness. The practice of Curanderismo teaches that the Mal de Ojo or Evil Eye can cause sickness.

Prayer and Ritual: These serve as tools for human interaction with the supernatural. Responders may encounter patients who are praying or performing rituals to attain good health.

Sacred Objects and Places: Religious objects may be used in concert with ritual and prayer to interact with the supernatural. Objects may also be worn by patients to protect them from harm. Some geographical locations may be considered sacred by patients, such as altars and ritual circles. These areas are typically used for sacred ceremonies.

Religious Experience, Such as Awe and Mysticism: Religion serves as a very personal concept to all of those who believe in it. The freedom to observe or not observe a religion is a personal choice that is extremely valuable. Religious experiences are personal or communal, and are the time when practitioners have a form of interaction with the supernatural. You may discover patients who are involved in a ritual or ceremony that produces this spiritual interaction.

Institutionalized Social Sharing of Some of These Traits: Responders may discover that a patient is calling for assistance from a priest or priestess. The organized social sharing of a religion may be called a church or a temple. This is where the patient learns about his/her religion and shares in this fellowship with fellow believers.

Anthropological Terms

Listed below are a few anthropological terms used frequently in this book. These terms refer to anthropological concepts that explain religious culture.

Artifacts: Objects produced by a specific culture. An example that responders may encounter is the iron cauldron known as Oggun in the Afro-Caribbean religion of Santeria.

Deities: The gods of a people. An example that responders may encounter when working with patients from the Haitian Voodoo community is the veneration of gods known as the Loa.

Myth: A story from or about the past that is told and retold in order to express certain values (or truths). An example that responders may encounter when meeting members of the Santeria community is the use of myths known as Patakis. These stories communicate instruction about the types of offerings that specific deities may ask for. For instance, a myth about the Santeria deity Eleggua tells of his need to have coconuts placed on his shrine.

Pantheon: A catalog of deities. The various magico-religious cultures may have specific terms that are used to denote the deities, such the Loa of Voodoo, the Orishas of Santeria and the Mpungu of Palo Mayombe.

Ritual: Symbolic behavior associated with religion or magic that is repetitive, sequential, nonordinary and believed to be powerful. Responders may encounter rituals in progress, such as the ritual known as Drawing Down the Moon in the religion of Wicca or an initiation ritual known as Kariocha in Santeria.

Symbol: Image used to express ideas too complex to explain directly. Responders may discover tattoos, ritual scarring or jewelry that contains symbols, such as the pentagram used by Wiccans, or the various symbols used to drive away Mal de Ojo or the Evil Eye in Hispanic folk religions.

Taboo: A cultural rule of avoidance. Responders should understand that recognition of taboo rules can affect how they should handle patient artifacts and how some patients are administered healthcare. An example that responders may encounter is the removing of the sacred beads known as Elekes in the Santeria religion or the avoidance of touching the artifacts that adorn the altar of a Wiccan practitioner.

Worldview: How someone interprets the world and how it works. Worldview governs the way that someone interprets life and how they react to this view. An example that responders may encounter includes the practitioners of Hispanic folk religions that believe a particular sickness may be caused by spiritual interference or jealousy from another individual.

Magico-Religious Cultures

This book focuses on religions commonly referred to as Occult or Magico-Religious cultures. *Magic* is a term used in a number of religious cultures to denote the use of supernatural techniques to achieve a specific desire. Magic may be referred to by a specific cultural name, such as Mana or Ache. Practitioners believe magic may be created by performing various techniques, such as prayer and ritual. Each religious culture has its own specific criteria in creating magic. The magico-religious worldview focuses on the world being dominated by various spiritual forces, and fate is usually determined by these spiritual forces. Disease and health also may be determined by spiritual forces. An understanding of this worldview will help you as a responder to be sensitive to the needs of those who share this belief.

Contemporary pop culture uses the colors of black and white to describe the intent or purpose of magic. In movies and television, White magic is depicted as being a benevolent force that is used to heal and protect the innocent. Black magic is commonly ascribed to those who dabble in curses and malevolent powers. While there are some authentic practitioners of magico-religious faiths that may use these terms, the majority of magical practitioners do not use them. In the magico-religious worldview, the same magic that is used to heal a sick child can be used to curse an enemy. Some practitioners have even likened magic to electricity, stating that both can be used for positive or negative results.

Some religious scholars have called magic "man's earliest attempt at technology." The use of drums, chanting, dancing and singing by primitive societies to create change is a universal phenomenon. Contemporary magical practices appear to fall into one of two categories. The first is called Theurgy. Theurgy is magic practiced to invoke the actions of a deity and ultimately to unite with that deity. Simply stated, this is magic performed to grow closer to a god. An example of this is the observance of Trance Possession in many of the magico-religious faiths in which the gods are called on to interact with humanity.

The second type of magical practice is known as Thaumaturgy. Thaumaturgy is "practical magic" that is performed to influence everyday events. A practitioner might perform a protection ritual to protect him from being robbed or he may pray for financial success.

In order to interact with the supernatural and obtain magic, the patient may use objects to summon this power. There are two universal concepts that dictate how a patient would use these objects. The first concept is known as The Law of Contact. This philosophy works on the principle that any item that has been in contact with someone can still affect that person (Figure 2.2). An example that responders may discover is the use of hair, nails or clothing kept on an altar in a patient's home. These objects may represent the focus of

Figure 2.2 The magical Law of Contact at work. The shoes are being used to conduct magical operations toward the owner of the shoes. The creator of this "working" was performing spell work to stop a man from abusing his wife.

the magical working. The second concept is known as The Law of Similarity. This works on the belief that any object that resembles someone can affect that person. Responders may discover objects, such as dolls or photographs that contain names or images, that resemble the target of magic

In the chapters to follow, we will look at some of the active magico-religious groups in the United States. The groups included are only a segment of the magico-religious community. They are listed because of the great number of practitioners. In each section we will look at the history and origins of these cultures in order to give you an overview into their past. And, we will look at theology and social structure in order to help you understand how to better communicate with these groups. We also will discuss physical objects, such as altars, artifacts and sacred spaces, in order to assist one in avoiding violating sacred taboos. Finally, we will look at the role that worldview plays in the health and healing process in the lives of practitioners and how your understanding can bring about a successful interaction.

References

1. National Center for Cultural Competence, Georgetown University Center for Child and Human Development, Washington, D.C.: http://www11.georgetown.edu/research/gucchd/nccc/foundations/frameworks.html
2. Wittgenstein, Ludwig, *Philosophical Investigations* (3rd ed.). Prentice Hall, Upper Saddle River, NJ, 1999.

Neopaganism

3

Assessing the Scene

> You and your partner receive a call involving a male who is complaining of chest pains. The location of the call is in a rural farm area in your district. Upon arriving at the scene, you find a group of approximately ten to fifteen men and women dressed in colorful robes. The group is standing in a circle formation. At the top of the circle is a table covered with various items, including candles, shells, cups and flowers. The smell of burning incense hangs in the air. As you approach, a man standing inside the circle holds up a knife and begins to rotate it around the circle. He shouts, "I banish this circle and thank the gods and goddesses that attended our rite. So mote it be." The group responds loudly by saying, "So mote it be." The group begins to step out of the circle and you then observe the person who is suffering chest pains.

The initial encounter that a first responder may have with a Wiccan religious ceremony may be puzzling. Someone who is unfamiliar with the cultural artifacts, rituals and practices of Wicca may confuse this religion with Satanism. Due to inaccuracies in the news media and with the similarities in artifacts, Wicca is many times falsely aligned with satanic beliefs. It is understandable that the appearance of robed figures, burning candles and ritual knives may appear threatening to an outsider, and it is possible that this may affect the manner in which the first responder communicates with the "mysterious" group.

Beliefs and Practices

The religion of Wicca, also known as witchcraft, is a religion that followers say has ancient roots in Pre-Christian Europe. Wicca or the Craft of the Wise comes from the early practices of a religion known as Paganism.

Paganism focuses on the worship of nature and the gods and goddesses who rule over the aspects of human nature and the environment. The term *pagan* comes from an Old English word *pagani*. The Pagani were country dwellers who held onto folk practices involving healing, agriculture and religion. Also known as Heathens (which simply means "one who lived on the heath"), this early culture believed that the forces of nature could be destructive or beneficial. There was a belief that if humans and nature could be "in tune" with each other, then man could live peacefully and successfully. Magic was simply the harnessing of the power of nature.

Early Pagans observed the phases of the moon and it's affect on crops and human behavior. Female Pagans also included midwives, who assisted in the delivery of children. Men would call on the God of the Hunt before they went out to kill the much-needed game for food. Pagan society would call on various gods and goddesses for successful crops in order to feed their families.

Paganism suffered a blow from the onslaught of the Medieval Inquisition. Followers of the Old Religion were driven underground; however, years later, Paganism experienced a revival of sorts in the Western world.

Neopaganism

While a number of Pagans seek to revive the old religions, some Pagans believe that they never actually died, but were secretly kept alive through the centuries. Surprisingly, these Pagan cultures claim to have a lineage that can be connected back to the original ancient cultures of Paganism.

Today Neopaganism is used as an umbrella term to describe a variety of magico-religious cultures. While these cultures have distinctive characteristics, they have some common elements as well. They tend to focus on preserving and being in tune with nature. They tend to be polytheistic, which means they follow many deities. They also tend to be somewhat secretive. While secrecy may seem to allude to something diabolical, it is observed as a way to preserve the purity of sacred rituals and teachings.

Contemporary Neopaganism encompasses a number of religions, including:

Asatru: A revival of the religions of the Europeans prior to encounters with Christianity. The word *Asatru* comes from the words True to the Aesir. The Aesir are the gods and goddesses of the Norse (Scandinavians from the Viking Age to today).

Druidism: The followers of this spiritual path follow the teachings and rituals of the Celtic Druids.

Shamanism: A technique that is practiced in a number of world cultures. Specific "gifted" individuals known as Shamans are believed to have access to hidden spiritual worlds through dreams and rituals. The practices of these cultures have been organized into a modern-day religious faith.

Wicca: The revival or continuation of the practices of European witchcraft. Wicca focuses on the worship of a female deity called The Goddess (Figure 3.1) and a male consort called The Great Horned God.

Figure 3.1 Responders may observe images of female deities from a number of world religions used to represent the Goddess of the Wiccan religion.

These are just a few of the many religious faiths that make up contemporary Neopaganism.

It is likely that responders will encounter Wicca more frequently than some of the other Neopagan faiths simply because of its larger population size. For this reason, we will focus primarily on Wicca.

History of Wicca

In the 1920s, an archaeologist named Margaret Murray published two books entitled *The Witch Cult in Western Europe* and *The God of the Witches*. Murray's hypothesis was that European witches were part of a surviving lineage of folk magicians. Murray's research was heavily disputed by historians and anthropologists; however, this did not stop her theories from affecting Western society. Many people became fascinated with the thought of connecting to something ancient and powerful.

In 1949, Englishman Gerald Gardner published a book called *High Magic's Aid*. Written under the guise of fiction, this book relayed actual cultural information about the practices of Wicca. The book served as a springboard for many Westerners to seek out information about the real world of Wicca and it's exotic practices. Gardner later wrote *Witchcraft Today*,[1] which was the first mass-published nonfictional work on Wicca. He is recognized as the founder of Gardenarian Wicca, a specific tradition/interpretation of Wicca.

Today there are hundreds of Wiccan traditions followed throughout the world, each serving as an interpretation of ancient Pagan practices. Similar to the denominations found in Judeo–Christian religions, Wiccan traditions have distinct histories, rituals, symbols and artifacts.

Traditions

There are several other traditions or interpretations of Wicca. Following are some of the more popular forms of Wicca found in North America.

Alexandrian Wicca

This tradition was founded by Alex Sanders, who claims to have been initiated by his grandmother in the early 1930s. Alexandrian Wicca uses very complex rituals and may use ritual nudity in ceremonies.

British Traditional Wicca

BTW, as it is called in the culture, is a term that denotes that a group can trace its lineage back to Wiccan Gerald Gardner or Alex and Maxine Sanders.

Celtic Wicca

Celtic Wicca focuses on the pantheon of deities and the practices of Druidic society of the British Isles.

Dianic Wicca

Dianic traditions focus on the superiority of females and the power of the goddess found in women. Dianic Wicca has been called Feminist Wicca by some critics.

Eclectic Wicca

This is a path that is open to many faiths. Followers take deities, rituals and philosophies from different religious traditions. The initiate is not bound to a particular dogma or rule.

Gardenarian Wicca

Founded by Gerald Gardner (see above), Gardenarian Wicca is perhaps one of the most practiced Wiccan traditions in North America. Gardenarian

Wicca focuses on worship of the god and goddess while holding the goddess as the more powerful deity. Members learn tradition through the texts known as the *Book of Shadows*, which was a diary and manual of worship given to the founder, which he passed on to his followers.

Georgian Wicca

This tradition was started in Bakersfield, California, in 1971 by George Patterson. The tradition takes elements from Gardenarian, Alexandrian traditions and from other recognized traditions. Members of this faith are encouraged to learn from all forms of magico-religious traditions.

Hereditary Wicca

Many American witches have traced their lineage back to generational witches. Spells and rituals have been passed down to them orally and through texts. While a Wiccan may belong to a "fam trad" (family tradition), he/she also may belong to a current tradition to identify with other believers.

Mohsian Tradition

Started in the 1960s as Eclectic American Tradition, Mohsian draws inspiration from Gardenarian Wicca, European shamanism and Celtic influences.

Strega Tradition

Italian witchcraft, known as Stregheria, has traditionally been followed by generational practitioners. However, there has been a new interest in the subject by those Americans unaffiliated with any kind of Italian traditions. Raven Grimassi is an Italian American that has popularized Strega tradition through such books as *Ways of the Strega* (2000, Llewellyn Publ.) and *The Book of the Holy Strega* (1981, Nemi Enterprises).

Beliefs

Wiccans seek to live in harmony with the Earth, which is viewed as a living entity. The primal elemental forces of Earth, wind, water and fire are viewed as powers to be honored, respected and sometimes controlled.

According to Wiccan theology, the universe is comprised of four elements: Earth, Wind, Water and Fire, which are said to be evident in all creation. Responders may see these elements represented on altars and in rituals they encounter when answering an emergency call. The most popular symbol used in Wicca is the pentagram; a visual representation of the elements in the form of a five-pointed star. The fifth point represents spirit.

While there is no sacred text central to Wicca, such as a Bible, there are several sacred texts, such as the *Book of Shadows,* used by members of the

Gardenarian tradition. Most Wiccan practices are communicated by oral tradition and the supplementing of various cultural texts.

Deities of Wicca

Wicca teaches that there are many gods that deserve reverence and worship. The primary deity is the goddess. The goddess is said to have been present in many different forms throughout history. Isis of Egyptians, Diana of the Romans and the Venus of the Greeks are just a few of the goddesses in history.

The goddess is referred to as the Lady in Wiccan circles. She is associated with the moon and is also identified as having three stages of existence: maiden, mother and crone.

The male deity that is worshipped in Wicca is known as the Horned God. Also known as The Lord, the Horned God represents the male element of deity and nature. His image is denoted by the wearing of horns (the horns *do not represent the character of Satan).* Many historians feel that we get the modern image of a horned "devil" from this early Pagan deity. The Horned God has been represented in many different world religions. Wiccans may call upon the deities of any spiritual tradition that they wish, such as Pan, the Greek god of the woodlands; Cerrounous, the Celtic god of fertility and the underworld; or even Herne, the hunter spirit of Britain. Therefore, responders may encounter an altar with statues of Buddha, Isis, Jesus and Hindu gods. Wiccans may use a pantheon of deities to worship and spiritually call upon. One occult historian summed it up like this: "All gods are one god, all goddesses are one goddess."

Ethics

The ethics of Wicca are iterated in a cultural phrase known as The Wiccan Rede. The word *rede* is Anglo-Saxon for *wise counsel.* The rede states the focus and boundaries of this magico-religious belief system. The rede (or counsel) says, "An ye harm none, do what thou wilt." The rede is similar to the Golden Rule in that it teaches Wiccans to show respect toward others in the practices of the religion.

Many Wiccans subscribe to the concept of karma. Karma is a concept originally taught in Eastern religions that describes the action of cause and effect. Karma teaches that anything that you do will return to affect you. If you are kind to others, you will be blessed with kindness. If you are destructive toward others, destruction will come to you. Karma is said to return three times as potent. In Wicca, this term is known as the Law of Three-Fold. This also affects the life and death process because many Wiccans believe in reincarnation. Reincarnation teaches that after death the soul is reborn or

Figure 3.2 A High Priestess places a cord around the initiate. This represents a "degree" of initiation in the Alexandrian Wiccan tradition.

migrates into a different body or being. Those who create "bad karma" will be reborn as lower beings as punishment.

Group Structure

The traditional term used to describe a Wiccan religious body is *coven*. Some groups use *circle*, *grove* or *order.*

Wiccans believe that anyone can interact with the gods; therefore, clergy is not necessary to access the gods. However, clergy is recognized as a respected and honored office. Traditional leadership in the coven is led by the High Priestess (HPS). The title of High Priestess is bestowed on the female who reaches a predetermined level of experience and initiation in the Craft. Each tradition has its own requirements for the position of High Priestess (Figure 3.2).

The High Priestess serves as the leader of the coven activities and rituals. She serves as counsel and guide to her initiates. Many members of this clergy wear necklaces made from amber or jet stones. Some traditions will recognize the High Priestess by a custom garter that she may wear or keep in her home.

Covens may have several other offices, such as officers who are craftmakers for the group and members who act as summoners carrying out spiritual tasks for the group. Selected members also may act as treasurers and oversee the funds of the coven.

Responders may encounter Wiccan security members known as *watchers*. Watchers are posted outside of ritual areas to intercept hostile or friendly outsiders who happen to come near the site. It is not uncommon to see watchers wearing two-way radios or self-defense weapons. Responders should ask for cooperation in locating the patient or scene that needs attention. Watchers may be able to assist in crowd control from unwanted visitors. Some large Pagan gatherings even have medical staff who are either members of the local Pagan community or who are familiar with the community.

Ritual Tools

Wiccans use a number of ritual tools in observance of rituals and worship, such as:

Athame: The blade used in a Wiccan ritual is a symbol of the Horned God. The blade is known as the *athame*. Some Wiccans prefer to use a sword for this tool. The traditional athame is a black-handled knife that is used to create sacred space and to banish energy. It is not for cutting animal or human flesh.

Bell: A bell may be used to cleanse the ritual environment. It may also be rung to end the ritual.

Boliene: Some Wiccans use a white-handled knife known as the *boliene*. The boliene is used to cut herbs and to carve candles and wood.

Book of Shadows: A book known as the *Book of Shadows* may be found on an altar. The name comes from the time in history when witches faced death and hid their secrets and spells "in the shadows." The book may belong to an individual or may be owned by the group.

Censer: The censer is a lamp used to burn incense. It may be attached to a chain that can be used to swing the lamp and spread the incense.

Chalice: The chalice is a cup that may be made from glass, clay or silver. The cup is used to represent the womb of the female deity. The chalice may be filled with water, wine or juice. It is used in rituals where it may be combined with the blade to represent male and female or it may be used to hold libations for the gods. A substance, such as wine, may be kept in the chalice to symbolize the fertility of the Earth. Herbal potions may also be created in the chalice.

Cords: Cords may be used by Wiccans in a form of magic known as "cord magic." The most popular use is for the cord to show the status of initiates in the coven. The cord may be different colors to show the level of initiation.

Pentacle: The pentacle is a round plate that is made of wood or stone. The plate usually contains symbols that represent the god and goddess, the ritual scourge, the ritual kiss, the second and third degrees, and the elements. The pentacle is used to "charge" some tools and may be used to hold the cakes used in rituals.

Scourge: The scourge (or cat o' nine tails) is a small whip used to symbolize several concepts in Wicca. It may be used to represent female dominance or it may be used to teach that wisdom is only available through pain and discipline. Some traditions use the scourge in a ritual scourging that occurs during initiation rites.

Wand: The wand is used to direct energy much like the athame. It is traditionally made from wood and may be decorated with crystals and sacred words carved into its side.

Tools may be consecrated and given magical properties. "Charging" tools may be done by placing ritual tools on altars and in sacred spaces. It is important that responders recognize that tools and jewelry may be "charged" and set apart for a sacred ritual.

Rituals and Ceremonies

While rituals may change according to the tradition and the practitioner, some of them are considered universal in Wiccan circles:

- Correspondences
- Preparation of ritual area
- Consecration of ritual tools and implements
- Casting the circle
- Calling the quarters
- Invocation of the deity
- Energy raised
- Spellwork
- Cakes/wine
- Opening and banishment of circle

Correspondences

The timing in which a ritual is performed is very important to Wiccan practice. It is a common magical belief that certain calendar dates, hours of the days, colors, scents and planets are all connected. Many Wiccans work all of these elements into the ritual. Before any rituals are performed, a Wiccan may need to wait until all of these aspects have occurred. It is also believed that some days of the year have more power then others. Rituals may be specifically held on these days to give the rituals more power. A ritual area may contain items that are specifically colored to represent these elemental correspondences. These colors are universal symbols of the elements. Some common color correspondences are

Air	=	Blue
Fire	=	Red
Water	=	Green
Earth	=	Yellow, Black or Brown

Preparation of Ritual Area

The tools and altar may be set up in a specific location of a house or outdoor area. Many traditions place the altar to the East or the North.

Consecration of Ritual Tools and Implements

The tools and ritual area may be cleaned with salt to purify them of negative energies. The ritual area is swept with a broom to cleanse the space for the ceremony. The area may also be purified with saltwater. Some may remove all the elements around the area to cleanse it while a chant or prayer is performed over the tools to consecrate them. Ritual tools are passed through the smoke of the censer to cleanse them. Then they are passed through a candle flame, sprinkled with water and rubbed with salt or dirt. This puts the tool through all of the elements.

Grounding

Grounding is establishing a connection to the energies of the Earth. It is said to keep the body from overstressing during the end of the ritual. It returns excess energy to the Earth. The practitioner may place the athame on the ground to place the energy back into the Earth.

Casting the Circle

The Wiccan must open an area for spiritual work. This is accomplished by "casting" a circle. The Wiccan uses his/her finger, a dagger, a sword, or a wand to create a wall of spiritual energy. This wall is created by the Wiccan walking clockwise (called *deosil*) and pointing the object used to direct energy. Although the movement is in a circle motion, the circle of energy is actually described as a "sphere" that encompasses the space. The circle is not to be broken during ritual because it is the sacred space in which the deities of Wicca manifest.

If the circle is to be broken, a doorway will be cut to let the practitioner walk outside the sacred space. This is cut open by the practitioner raising the athame and moving it counterclockwise (*widdershins*) and tracing a door.

Calling the Quarters

The directions of North, South, East and West are protected by guardian spirits, which are sometimes called *watchtowers*. The directions or quarters are called to witness the ritual. The Wiccan may draw or "invoke" a pentagram in the air that represents the quarter and the element it represents. The watchers are called by specific prayers. A traditional call is

> "All ye mighty Lords and Ladies of the Watchtowers of North, bring forth the Earth Mother. The Gardener of the Earth, so that she may witness the purification of our bodies with this salt and plant the seed of spiritual growth within our souls."

Greek names for the four winds may be used during the calls. These spirits are sent away and thanked at the end of the ritual.

Invocation of Deity

The deity is called and invited to appear in the circle. The god may be called by many names, such as Cerrounos, Pan, Horned God, or Herne, the Hunter. The goddess may be called Diana, Hecate, Isis or Cerridwen of the Cauldron. An example of an invocation follows:

> Gracious Goddess,
> You who are the Queen of the Gods,
> The lamp of night,
> The Creator of all that is wild and free;
> Mother of woman and man;
> Lover of the Horned One, and Protector of all the Wicca:
> Descend, I pray,
> With Your Lunar ray of Power
> Upon my circle here!

Energy Is Raised

Energy is raised through singing, chanting, dancing or drumming, and is contained within the magickal* circle. This energy is then raised into a cone of power, which then can be channeled to a specific area of concentration to perform magic. The cone of power is easily visualized by picturing a traditional witch.

Spellwork

Spellwork is done with the energy raised. Spells are performed for healing, protection, spiritual peace, and other wishes.

Cakes/Wine

The ingestion of wine and cakes will bring the Wiccan out of the ritual state of mind. This also binds the practitioners through the sharing of food. The food is typically consecrated by the High Priestess and High Priest.

Opening and Banishment of the Circle

The circle must be banished after the ritual. The Wiccan walks counterclockwise (called *widdershins*) to take the energy away. This will open the ritual area and allow the Wiccan to leave the sacred space. The deities and guardians are released.

The closing of a circle is usually met with the cry: "Merry meet, merry part, and merry meet again."

Rites of Passage

Wiccaning: This ritual presents a child to the deities of Wicca. The child may be presented to the Elemental Watchers. The child is traditionally anointed on the head with a touch of oil. The child may receive a Wiccan name during this ceremony.

Coming of Age: Some covens will observe a Coming of Age ritual when a girl begins her menstrual cycle.

Handfasting: The handfasting is a wedding ceremony. The man and woman are joined by hands to dedicate themselves and to the gods. The ceremony

* The spelling with the terminal "k" was repopularized in the first half of the twentieth century by Aleister Crowley when he made it a core component of his mystical system of Thelema.

may be marked by a completion of the ritual The Great Rite. The handfasting is legally binding if the priest or priestess is legally ordained.

Funeral Rites: The loss of a coven member may be recognized by a ceremony held strictly in private by fellow coven members. The concept of a Pagan paradise, known as the Summerlands, is held by many with the Wiccan worldview. One ritual act may be the "breaking of the bowl."

Holy Days

Wiccans may gather on specific times to perform rituals and socialize. Wiccan traditions encourage gatherings during certain phases of the moon. These gatherings are called Esbats. The word *esbat* is French for "to frolic." The moon is revered because of its representation of the goddess as well as its importance to nature. Public Esbats may be advertised in metaphysical supply stores and on Internet Web sites.

Sabbats are considered the Wiccans high holy days. Many of them correspond with changes of the seasons. Traditionally, there are eight Sabbats celebrated by Wiccans. The greater Sabbats are Imbolc, Beltane, Lughnassad, and Samhain. The lesser Sabbats are the summer and winter solstices, and the autumnal and spring equinoxes. These holidays are usually pictured as a wheel. The wheel contains the seasons and turns as time passes.

Each Sabbat has a specific ritual and symbolic meaning regarding the life and death of the gods.

Samhain

Samhain is celebrated October 31st. This is the celebration of the time of year when the veil between the worlds of the living and the dead are thinnest. Darkness is dominant. This is the New Year's Eve of the Celtic religions. The Horned God becomes the Lord over Summerland. This is the change from summer to winter.

Yule

Yule occurs around December 22. This is the winter solstice. Wiccans celebrate the longest night of the year as well as the rebirth of the Sun God. There is a fight between the Oak King and the Holly King.

Imbolc

The holiday of Imbolc occurs February 2. This celebrates the first appearance of light. Imbolc means *in the belly*. The goddess is recovering from giving birth to the god. The Sun God stays up longer during this time. This celebration is important to Brigid, the goddess of healing. The priestess may wear a crown of lights.

Ostara

Ostara, or the spring equinox, is celebrated March 21. This is the day of equal balance of day and night. Spring fertility is celebrated, as is Ostara, goddess of fertility. The Christian celebration of Easter is taken from this holiday. The goddess becomes pregnant by the Horned God.

Beltane

The Sabbat of Beltane is celebrated April 30. The holiday celebrates the changing of winter to summer. Maypoles are planted this day. The maypole celebrates the Earth's fertility. The wreath and pole symbolize fertility while the dancing around the pole builds energy to pass into the Earth.

Litha

Litha is the celebration of Midsummer's eve or summer solstice. It is usually held June 21. It is the longest day and shortest night of the year with the Sun God at his peak. This is a celebration of transformation. The Oak King dies and the Holly King is born.

Lammas

Lammas is celebrated July 31 through August 1. This is the time of harvest. The word *lammas* comes from Old English words that mean *loaf* and *mass.* It is an ancient celebration of the first fruits of harvest coming in. The Celtic Sun God, Lugh, is also revered on this date. The god begins to descend into the underworld.

Mabon

Mabon is celebrated September 21. This is the autumnal equinox. This is the sacrifice of the Sun God and a celebration of the balance between light and day. The autumn equinox marks the end of the harvest.

Sacred Spaces

Wiccan altars and sacred spaces are similar to pieces of art. They may be very simple with a few well-placed items or they may be very elaborate with custom-crafted tools and artifacts. A Wiccan altar may be as basic as a few pieces of stone, feathers and a cup of water, or it may be a handcrafted statue of a Roman goddess, with flowers, jewelry and candles. The important aspect is to remember that these sacred spaces mean something to the owner (Figure 3.3).

Some Wiccans will designate outdoor areas as sacred spaces. Rocks and trees may be recognized as natural objects that invoke the spiritual. Some Wiccans use their backyard as a sacred space to perform rituals.

Figure 3.3 A Wiccan altar. This altar contains objects that may appear as "non-religious" objects, such as the rocks, pinecones, plants and shells. Responders may observe what appear to be common objects such as these on altars and in shrines.

The altar is traditionally placed in the northern area of the sacred space. The direction of North is of significance to Wiccans because it represents the element of Earth. The Wiccan altar contains artifacts and substances that are used in ritual and worship. Some of the most commonly used objects include:

The Gods: Statues, masks, dolls and pictures are placed on altars to represent the god and goddess. Deer antlers and seashells may be used to represent the male and female element (Figure 3.4 and Figure 3.5).

The Elements: The altar may also contain objects that represent the four elements. Earth may be represented by pieces of soil, plants, dollar bills, stones or wood. Air may be represented by a feather, fan or bird's nest. Water may be represented by a bowl of water, seashells and even pictures of fish. Fire can be represented by an extra candle, red objects or an image of the sun. The elements may also be represented by colored candles. Fire may be represented by a red candle, water by a blue candle, Earth by a green candle, and air by a yellow candle.

Cauldron: The cauldron may be placed on the altar to represent the goddess. The cauldron may contain herbs or incense to burn during the ritual.

Salt: Salt may be placed on an altar to cleanse ritual spaces.

Offerings: Altars may contain candy, flowers, fruits and vegetables. These may be given as offerings to the gods.

Photographs: Altars may contain photos of relatives and friends that are seeking healing or have passed away. The photo may be present to show respect and honor to the ancestor or to communicate with the dead.

Figure 3.4 Upon entering a residence, responders may discover cultural objects related to a person's faith as decorations. The wreath in the window is the sacred Pentagram of the Wiccan faith, and the stone ram represents the Horned God of Neopagan Wicca.

Figure 3.5 Figures representing the God and Goddess of Wicca.

Note: Responders should avoid touching altars or handling objects found on altars.

Health and Sickness

There are a number of approaches to health and sickness in Wicca. The following are some of the more popular healing techniques employed by practitioners.

Cord Healing

A cloth cord may be worn by the patient. Feelings of sickness and thoughts of the illness may be focused into the cords. The cord is pulled away from the patient with the intent of removing the sickness.

Aromatherapy

Aromatherapy is the art of healing using oils and oil blends. The aroma of the oils reduces stress and anxiety.

Chanting

Chants are viewed as energized words used to raise "power" which can be used in healing. One Wiccan's *Book of Shadows* uses the following chant called "The Healing Rune":

> This is the spell that we intone
> Flesh to flesh and bone to bone
> Sinew to sinew and vein to vein
> And each one shall be whole again

Auric Healing

The aura is seen as the electromagnetic field that surrounds the body of all living beings. Humans, animals and plants all have this energy, which has spiritual, physical, mental and emotional qualities. The aura may be known as the "etheral body" and has different layers of colors, vibrations and even locations on the human body. Some Wiccans believe that the aura can be seen by gifted individuals. The color (or clarity) of the aura is an indicator of the health of the body. The following are a few examples of how these colors may be interpreted:

- Red auras show that someone has strong passion. Dark red may also indicate that the person is quick tempered.
- Orange auras express creativity or may also indicate kidney problems.
- Yellow auras characterize optimism or good health.
- Green auras indicate sympathy or denote someone with healing abilities.

- Blue auras signify calmness, but also indicate moodiness or depression.
- Black auras signify no conscience or may denote a sociopath.
- White auras characterize purity and truth.

Some believe the aura is the first area that is attacked when sickness attacks the body. Sickness may be the result of loss or imbalance in the aura. The energy, sometimes called Prana, is manipulated and the patient is "recharged" with energy from outside sources. This technique of healing may include the laying on of hands (Figure 3.6).

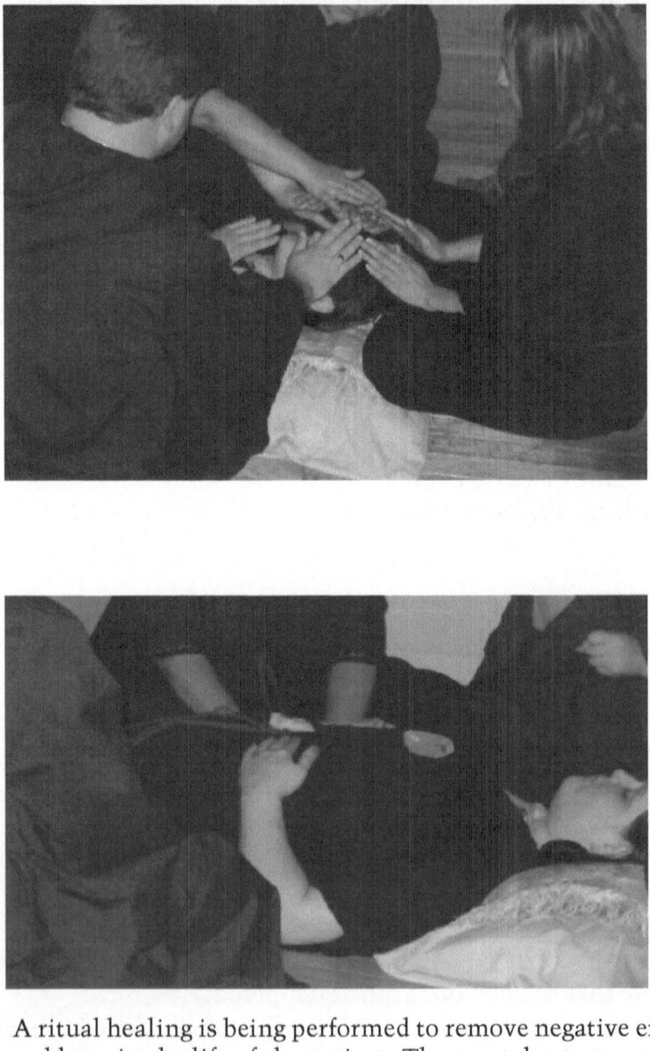

Figure 3.6 A ritual healing is being performed to remove negative energies that are causing problems in the life of the patient. The crystal acts as a conductor of energy.

Chakras

Chakras are said to be energy points located throughout the human body. These points are the locations through which energy is distributed throughout the cells, tissues and organs.

The "root chakra" is the line of energy that runs from the feet to the lowest part of the abdomen. This is the energy area that provides survival and grounding powers. This chakra coincides with the gonad glands.

The "navel chakra" is found in the area of sexual reproduction and embodies creativity. This chakra coincides with the adrenal gland.

The "solar plexus chakra" is located exactly where it indicates and deals with the will, energy and power. This chakra coincides with the lyden gland.

The "heart chakra" covers the heart and lung area and encompasses the realms of love and lust. This chakra coincides with the thymus gland.

The "throat chakra" covers the throat and larynx area as well as the glands around them, and covers communication. This chakra coincides with the thyroid gland.

The "third eye chakra" is located between the eyes and involves mental energy and focus. This chakra coincides with the pineal gland.

The "crown chakra" is found at the tip of the head and protects against negative forces. This chakra coincides with the pituitary gland.

The misalignment of these energy points can produce sickness. Techniques involving sound therapy, massage and meditation are used to align these points.

Absent Healing

If a person is sick and the fellowship group is unavailable to physically visit them, a coven may send healing energy from a distance through various healing rituals. The group may focus on a photo or an image in the form of a doll to create healing for the patient. Altars may contain hair, clothing and other materials to be used in sympathetic magic rituals.

One spell calls for the use of a "stand-in"; a person who resembles the patient. He or she is viewed as a model of the patient and healing rituals are performed on this person with hopes that they will benefit the patient.

Herbalism

Wiccan writers Janet and Stewart Farrar tell us that Wiccans are drawn to herbalism because "the Craft is a Nature-based religion, and the study of herbs is a very fruitful way of sharpening their attunement to Gaia, the Earth organism, on all the levels."[2]

Responders may discover that a patient has ingested herbs or applied them to wounds. The use of herbs by Wiccans has two facets. The first is the traditionally recognized properties of medicine as observed by most Westerners. The second is concerned with magical energies that herbs may produce. Some traditional practitioners use the term *Wortcunning* to describe the secret knowledge of herbs and their magical properties.

Herbs may be used in a number of ways, such as ingested or placed in water as a tea, or they may be placed in bathwater. The practitioner sits in the bath and takes in the medicinal and magical properties through his/her skin. Herbs also can be carried as charms. Commonly found in small bags, the herb provides a transportable power, such as protection or healing. Herbs may also be placed in oils. The oil provides a liquid form of the herb to be used to anoint persons and objects with its powers. Herbs may also be smoked in pipes and rolling papers. Typically, smoking an herb is used to create altered states of consciousness. Herbs can also be simply placed in ritual areas in order to draw magical energies to these locations.

Herbs used for magical practices may have the potential to be dangerous if ingested. Some common herbs used in Wiccan magic include:

Mandrake (*Atropa mandragora*): Folk names include Deadly Nightshade, Devil's Apple and Herb of Circe. The root of the mandrake resembles the shape of a human being and can be carried as an amulet of protection. The root also can be kept in a house to protect the dwelling. Some literature suggests soaking the root in spring water to "wake" it. A tea may be made with the root to produce visions.

Angelica (*Angelica archangelica*): Folk names include Masterwort and Garden Angelica. This legendary herb is alleged to have been given to man by an archangel to cure the plague. The herb is used to heal sickness and is believed to magically protect the owner of the root. Pieces may also be dried and burned as incense. Angelica added to bathwater can remove a hex. Large doses can produce high blood pressure and raise the heart rate.

Thyme (*Thymus vulgaris*): Folk names include Garden Thyme. The herb is used to guard against nightmares. It may be placed inside a pillow to prevent these events. Thyme may also be burned as incense or worn as an amulet to guard against sadness or to draw love. Thyme is also used in cleansing rituals to remove negative energies.

Sandalwood (*Santalum album* or *Santalum rubrum*): Folk names include Red Sanders. Sandalwood is used to create a spiritual environment. The herb is used to increase power in performing the magical practices of divination, astral travel and working with spirits.

Hemlock (*Conium maculatum*): Folk names include Poison Hemlock, Poison Parsley, Herb Bennet and Corobane. Hemlock is historically recognized as a poison and as an ingredient used in flying ointment. Hemlock assisted early witches in the practice of astral travel; however, legends rumored that witches could actually fly. Many Wiccans use the herb in purification rituals.

Nettle (*Urtica diocia*): Folk names include Stinging Nettle, Greater Nettle and Common Nettle. The most common nettle found in the United States is the stinging nettle, which has fine hairs that contain an acid solution. Contact with skin can produce burning and irritation. The herb can be dried and used as a protective amulet and also placed in a home as a form of protection.

Mugwort (*Artemisia vulgaris*): Folk names include Artemis herb, Artemisia, St. John's Plant, and Naughty Man. Made into a tea, Mugwort increases clairvoyance.

Arabic gum (*Acacia senegal/Acacia seyal*): May be in a resin or powder form. The substance is used to purify. The ritual use of Arabic gum may be to draw protective circles and to open psychic channels.

Basil (*Ocimum basilicum*): May be called St. Joseph's Wort and Witches Herb. Basil is used in spellwork concerning prosperity and wealth. Basil made into a tea can ease nausea.

Benzoin (*Styrax benzoin*) Benzoin is burned to purify a space. The resin may be burned to assist in astral travel.

Chamomile (*Anthemis noblis*): Folk names include Ground Apple, White Star and Scented Mayweed. Chamomile is used in rituals for peace and relaxation. Teas and baths may be made using this herb.

Fennel (*Foeniculum vulgare*): Fennel can be used for protection and banishing negative energies.

Frankincense (*Boswellia* genus): Frankincense may be known as Olibanum and Frankincense Tears. This resin is burned to purify an area and for protection.

Vervain (*Verbena officinalis*): Folk names include Juno's Tears, Herb of Grace and Pigeon Grass. Vervain is used to assist in divination and prophecy.[3]

Ritual Body Art

Some Wiccan circles make use of ritual body paint to aid in the healing process. Ritual body art uses various colors and sacred symbols as a means of communication to society and to the deities. A pregnant woman may have her stomach painted with a green triangle surrounding a circle. The color green standing for fertility and the symbols standing for pregnancy.

Smudging

The practice of smudging has historically been connected to the Native Americans. Smudging was a technique used to remove negative energies from a person and from a place in order to create a sacred environment. Wiccans may burn dried herbs in a bowl or shell. The herbs can also be tied together in a bundle. The herbs produce a smoke that is fanned around the area being cleansed. A feather is commonly used to fan the smoke. Wiccans also may smudge themselves or others with herbs in a cleansing ritual.

Sage is a commonly burned herb used in smudging. Responders may discover that the scent of burning sage is similar to the scent of burning marijuana.

Candles

Candles may be used in healing rituals and they come in a number of shapes, sizes and colors. Some of the common attributes of candle colors include:

- Black: evil, protection, adversity
- Blue: moodiness, peace, tranquility, health
- Brown: neutrality, uncertainty, doubt, balance
- Green: money, success, fertility, luck
- Orange: encouragement, attraction, joy
- Pink: love, honor, feminine
- Purple: power, tension, ambition
- Red: strength, love, passion, sex, vitality
- White: purity, truth, god, spirituality, clairvoyance
- Yellow: charm, confidence, creativity

Candles are traditionally anointed with oil. The practitioner chooses an oil that will enhance the power of the candle. The oil is then rubbed onto the candle in a particular pattern. It may be rubbed down the candle to draw in energy and rubbed away from the candle to get rid of energies. The practitioner may also carve symbols and the name of the person needing to be healed into the candle. Photos and names of patients may be placed under the candle for healing purposes (Figure 3.7).

One healing ritual consists of the lighting of candles while visualizing health for the ill. At the end of the ritual, the candle is extinguished. An example of a candle spell follows below.

Sample Candle Magic Spell

Materials needed: one pale blue candle and a pencil

Inscribe the candle with your health problem, then on top, superimpose a "7," the lower leg of which corkscrews from right to left to make three complete loops. Light the candle and visualize the affected area as bright red. Holding the image in your mind's eye, mentally paint the area a soft, cool, healing green. Then say something like:

Symbol that can cure all ills
And healing green, bend to my will
Eradicate the problem here
Cast off damage, cast out fear
And bring good health at once to me
As I will, so mote it be

Let the candle burn all the way down, and continue any medications prescribed by your healthcare practitioner.[4]

Figure 3.7 Candle magic is practiced in many different world religions. This candle is decorated with Theban, an alphabet that is commonly used by Wiccans.

Destruction of Illness

A spell may be performed in which an item representing the sickness is burned to magically destroy the sickness.

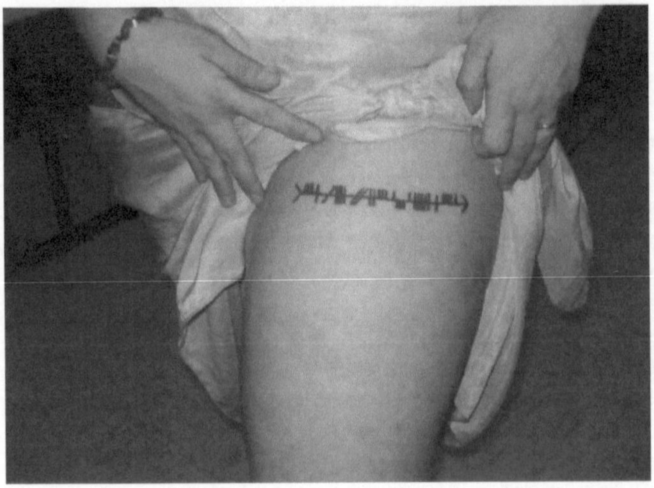

Figure 3.8 Responders may discover tattoos and ritual body art on patients.

Poppets: Poppets are dolls used to represent the target of a spell. Responders discovering these dolls may assume malevolent workings (à la Voodoo doll) are being performed. However, the poppet is used for *healing* rituals.

Ritual Body Art: It is believed that symbols communicate a need to the spiritual realm. Some Wiccans in need of healing may have various magical symbols and colors painted onto the face, neck, chest, breasts, thighs and back. Symbols may represent the protection of deities, emotions, such as happiness or mourning, and symbols for healing[5] (Figure 3.8).

Sweat Lodges: Some Wiccans utilize the Native American sauna known as the sweat lodge. Sweat lodges are typically domed-shaped huts constructed from tree branches and cloth or animal skin. The inner space of the dome contains stones that are heated in a fire. The door to the lodge is closed with the participant inside. The steam inside, combined with burning herbs, works to purify the occupants and place them in a spiritual state.

Articles of Comfort

Amulets: Amulets are objects that provide protection when worn or carried. They may be composed of gemstones, drawings, jewelry, herbs, bones and/or coins. Amulets may be in the pockets of clothing or worn on a necklace or bracelet.

Jewelry: Amulets and talismans may double as jewelry. Silver jewelry is worn to represent the goddess. The High Priestess may wear a necklace made from amber and jet gemstones to indicate their position in the

Craft. Animal bone or claws may be worn as protective amulets. Some traditions present the High Priestess with a ritual garter to indicate the number of covens that have "hived" off from her.

Stones: Stones link Wiccans with the Earth. Stones are believed to contain magical properties and can conduct energies much like a radio transmitter. Stones may be "charged" where energy is placed into the stones before they are worn. Some Wiccans cleanse stones in salt water to remove negative energies. Stones may be carried in bags or worn on necklaces.

Source of Sickness

Psychic attacks: Some Wiccans believe that they can be magically attacked by enemies. For protection, they may put a protective circle around themselves or make a pentagram in the air. Some Wiccans may keep crystals on their property as protection.

Cursed Objects: Some Wiccans believe that objects can be conductors of negative energy if used in malevolent rituals. A negatively charged item left on someone's property can produce illness.

Taboos

Responders encountering a group in ritual may need to enter the ritual space. Allow the group to advise you when it is safe to enter. This simply shows courtesy toward the group's cultural rules. Be aware that sweeping actions with the ritual tools may be used to banish the ritual space (Figure 3.9).

Do not disturb altars, shrines or ritual tools unless it is necessary for the health of the patient. If you have a question regarding items on the altar,

Figure 3.9 Responders may encounter rituals performed in outdoor settings. This ritual circle is located at the residence of a Wiccan High Priestess.

Figure 3.10 Responders should avoid touching shrines and altars.

such as incense, herbs or possible health-related hazards, ask other members at the scene to assist or ask the patient if it is okay to touch the articles (Figure 3.10).

Responder Issues

When encountering a group in ritual, realize that it may be awkward for the group to be seen in ritual. Some members of the group may not be public about their faith or they may have encountered negative reactions to their faith in the past. Respond in a kind and professional manner.

Many Wiccan events and celebrations take place outdoors. Members may encounter heat stroke from the sun, insect bites and rashes from plants. Most organized events will have someone designated to assist in medical emergencies. The typical gathering will have someone who is a Wiccan healthcare professional.

Some oils can become irritants if applied too heavily. Oil in the eyes of a patient can cause irritation and some oils are photosensitive and can cause sunburn if exposed to the sun for prolonged periods of time.

Allow the patient to carry any necessary objects of protection that may give him/her comfort, such as amulets, jewelry, talismans, gemstones, etc.

Be advised that some groups may observe their rituals within a confined ritual space. If herbs or incense are burned, this could cause difficulty in breathing for some members of the group. Some herbs like sage can be particularly overpowering in confined spaces.

Some Wiccan groups will observe sacred rituals in the nude. There is a possibility that responders could be called to the scene where a group is practicing "skyclad," a cultural term for ritual nudity.

Although it is not a common practice, some Wiccan groups will use a drop of blood from a member to take an oath of initiation. The blood represents the life force of man. This will usually be a very small amount, but the possibility always exists that the initiate could faint or loose too much blood if performed improperly.

There are some Wiccan traditions that may utilize the use of a cord to bind the arms of an initiate during certain initiation rites. This cord may be wrapped around the arms and around the neck. Although the intent is *not* to harm the initiate, it is possible that the cord could be tied too tight or tightened accidentally.

Some rituals may be performed to induce a trance state. Responders may encounter a victim who is in this state as a result of meditation, dancing or other forms of inducing trance. A person who acts as a medium for spiritual workings may also be in a trance state. If other members of the group are present, ask them to assist you in your communications with the victim.

During the celebration of Beltane, some Wiccans may decide to jump over the fire that is burning in the cauldrons used to mark the holiday. Practitioners could accidentally receive burns from these fires.

Responders may find health problems with Wiccans who use sweat lodges. Problems can occur involving heat exhaustion, dehydration and smoke inhalation.

Weapons/Harmful Implements

If a patient being treated is wearing an athame and you must remove the blade, advise the patient that the blade will be kept safe until medical care is completed. It is advisable to take notes of any items you may take from the patient.

References

1. Clifton, Charles S., *Witchcraft Today: Book One*, Llewellyn Publications, Woodbury, MN, 1992, p. 23.
2. Farrar, Janet and Stewart Farrar, *A Witches Bible Compleat*, Magickal Childe Publishing, Inc., New York, 1981, chap. 21.
3. Reith, Rev. Velvet, *Common Herbs for Use in Multicultural Religious/Healing Practices*, Tennessee IAI Conference, Ritualistic Crime Workshop, 2006.
4. Morrison, Dorothy, *Everyday Moon Magic*, Llewellyn Publications, Woodbury, MN, 2004.
5. Arnold, Charles, *Ritual Body Art: Drawing the Spirit*, Phoenix Publishing, Blaine, WA, 1987

Santeria (Regla de Ocha) 4

Assessing the Scene

> You receive a call regarding a female patient who has fallen and is injured. She is located on a hill overlooking a local river. As you approach the scene, you discover a Hispanic female wrapped in blue cloth lying on a bed of rocks. Her head is bleeding. She is conscious, but obviously startled. As you begin to administer aid to the woman, you notice a wooden raft at her feet. On the raft is a watermelon, candles, pennies and a dead chicken. Puzzled, you look at the patient and she tells you "It's my religion, don't worry."

Responders who encounter members of the Santeria religion may find a number of artifacts and rituals that appear much as Hollywood has portrayed Voodoo rituals in movies. However, a deeper analysis of Santeria reveals a complex system of beliefs, rituals and philosophies that convey a centuries-old religion.

Santeria is a religion practiced by over 20,000 Americans.[1] The religion was once observed in casual or consistent practice by members of only the Cuban, Puerto Rican and Mexican communities. However, there are now a number of ethnic groups that also practice the religion. Santeria is a "syncretic" religion that was developed through the interaction of African slaves and Catholic slaveholders. Syncretic religions seek to reconcile or mix practices of various religions. The use of syncretism allowed the religion of Santeria to survive through the horrors of slavery.

History of Santeria

The Santeria religion comes from the Yoruba people of West Africa. In the mid-sixteenth century, thousands of Yoruba people were kidnapped and taken as slaves. They were then transported to British, French, Spanish and Portuguese colonies in the Caribbean Islands to live and work on plantations as an enslaved populace. However, the West African slaves brought with them their Yoruba religious culture, but were eventually forced by their captors to abandon their religious obligation to the deities and to the practices of the African traditional religions.

To ensure the survival of their religion, the Yoruba slaves secretly kept their spiritual traditions alive. Meeting in houses known as Cabildos, the various groups could celebrate the rituals, songs and dances of their culture. The cabildos were identified by specific religious groups known as Regla. The Regla de Ocha was the "rule of the Orishas," a phrase still used today to denote contemporary Santeria. (The Orishas are the Yoruba deities worshipped in Santeria.) The Yoruba people found common elements in the Roman Catholic saints of the slave owners' religion and the indigenous deities of Africa. A syncretism between the saints of the Catholic Church and the African deities known as Orishas was formed. This allowed the Yoruba slaves to use the saints as camouflage while still observing their religion. The groups, who identified with this practice, were known as Lucumi. Today the religion is practiced in the open with the syncretism between Orisha and saints being continued as a cultural tradition. Some followers have referred to the saints as the "costumes" that the Orishas wear in the new world.

There is evidence that Santeria moved north of the border into the United States as early as 1946 when Francisco "Pancho" Mora migrated into the States and became the first recognized Babalawo (Santeria priest) in America. Mora established a temple in the Upper West Side of New York City. In 1959, another significant personality in Santeria history, named Walter King, traveled to Cuba to become initiated in the religion. King is noted as being the first African American to be initiated in the religion. Upon his return to the States, King changed his name to Oba Osejiman Adeummi and started the Yoruba Temple in New York City. In 1961, Mercedes Noble was ordained the first Santera (priestess of Santeria) in the United States. Noble, who was also known as Oban Yoko, opened a Casa de Santo (House of Saint), which became a location for ordination rites in the States.

The Mariel Boatlift of 1980 brought several thousand Cubans to the South Florida shores between April and October of that year. Some trepidation followed these Cubans as they flooded into the area. As Cuban refugees before them, the Mariel boat people brought with them their island culture and religious practices. One of the cultural aspects that became apparent to the public eye was the practice of Santeria. Numerous public service agencies began to share information regarding the use of hand tattoos, colored beads and bizarre rituals by the Cuban refugees. This was one of many early incidents that served to create the cloud of misunderstanding that still surrounds the religion today.

In 1992, Santeria practitioners from Hialeah, Florida protested local ordinances that banned ritual animal sacrifices by Santeria practitioners. This issue was taken to the United States Supreme Court where it was ruled that the city had specifically focused on Santeria and should have created a generalized ordinance that did not target a specific religious culture. The issue of animal sacrifice brought Santeria into the public spotlight where it received critical attention by an uneducated public. Santeria became equated by some with Satanism. A religion that developed from an African traditional culture that was no stranger to animal sacrifice was looked upon by the local media as a savage form of pagan worship.[2]

In order for responders to understand the secrecy surrounding Santeria, it is important to have the historical perspective. Many believers still wrestle with the stereotypes and prejudice that results from the media and Hollywood portrayals of the religion.

Beliefs and Practices

The primary focus of Santeria is to introduce humanity to the Orishas that operate in this world. Humans are children of the Orishas and each human being has a personal Orisha that they are called to serve. Humans feed the Orishas through sacrifices and provide earthly instruction to guide other humans into the service of the Orishas. The Orishas likewise provide spiritual power to humans known as Ache. Ache, which is spiritual energy, can reside inside believers as well as inside ritual implements.

The Deities of Santeria

The Yoruba deities worshipped in Santeria are known as Orishas.[3] According to Santeria mythology, the Orishas are manifestations of the creator deity known as Olodumare. The Orishas govern all aspects of nature and humanity. For instance, the Orisha Yemaya governs the ocean waters and the human aspects of maternity. Santeria myths, known as Patakis, are communicated orally to followers to explain the mechanics of the spiritual and physical worlds. The Patakis tell of the creator Olodumare (who owns heaven) and of his son Olofi. The Orishas Olodumare, Olofi and Olorun rule over the other Orishas, but are not directly worshipped. The lesser Orishas live in the material world and serve to protect humanity. The Orishas are similar to the gods and goddesses of the Greeks. Each one having his/her own favorite color, number, food, drum rhythm and tool (Figure 4.1).

The following are some of the more recognized Orishas in Santeria.

Elegua

Elegua is syncretized with Saint Anthony. Some houses may have Elegua represented by the Spanish statue of Nino Atocha, the Christ child. He is represented by a cement head with cowrie shells for the eyes, nose, and mouth. Elegua owns the keys to the spiritual realm and is called upon at the beginning of rituals to open the doorway to the spiritual world. The icon of Elegua may be found sitting on a terra cotta plate. This indicates stability. Responders

Figure 4.1 Shown are various ritual artifacts representing the deities of the Santeria religion. Many of these objects may be observed throughout the homes of practitioners. (Courtesy of Webb County Sheriff's Department, Laredo. Texas.)

Figure 4.2 A shrine to the Orisha Elegua. Offerings to the deity include candy, rum and money.

may see the icon of Elegua placed near doorways. His image may be found along with a red and black beaded stick with a crook and he may be wearing a small straw hat. His shrine may also contain toys and candy representing his childlike nature. He may have other manifestations in the forms of coconuts, seashells and large rocks (Figure 4.2).

Ogun

Ogun is syncretized with Saint Peter. He is the divine ironworker and patron of ironworkers. Ogun is represented by an iron cauldron filled with materials, such as iron spikes, chains and other implements. These items are typically covered in Corojo (palm oil) butter. Green and black colored items will be found in his shrine as well. Ogun's patron animal is the dog, so many shrines contain stuffed animals and statues of dog images. The ceremonial knife that is used to commit animal sacrifices is often placed inside the cauldron of Ogun.

Ochosi

Hunting and justice are governed by the god Ochosi. Ochosi is syncretized with Saint Norbert. He is represented by a small or large metal crossbow. Responders may see the crossbow of Ochosi hanging near the door to a home. Some shrines for Ochosi hold deer antlers and handcuffs. Ochosi artifacts may be violet in color.

Oshun

Oshun is syncretized with Our Lady of La Caridad del Cobre. She is the goddess of love and sexuality. She also governs matters of money and rules over the river waters. Her shrines contain materials made from copper, fans, mirrors, ducks and boats or other river-related items. Honey may be placed on the altar as well as apple cider. Her color is yellow.

Obatala

This Orisha is syncretized with Our Lady of Mercy. Obatala is the father of the Orishas, and is frequently referred to as Father of the White Cloth. Obatala is said to "own" the head of humans and is represented by anything white, such as cotton, doves and eggs.

Chango

This fiery Orisha is syncretized with Saint Barbara and represents fire, thunder and lightning. Chango was an actual king in Africa who was deified after his death. Chango's shrine contains his wooden double-bladed ax and sword. Images of Saint Barbara may be placed in homes to represent Chango. The statue may hold a sword that can be placed in an upward or downward position. It is said that the sword pointing upward represents a time of defense in the life of the statue's owner. Chango's colors are red and white (see Figure 4.3).

Oya

Oya is syncretized with Our Lady of Candelaria and Saint Theresa. Oya owns the cemeteries, winds and storms. Shrines to Oya contain masks, spears and nine copper bracelets. Her colors are maroon and nine various other colors. Her

Figure 4.3 A statue known as Chango Macho is used in spiritual workings. (Courtesy of Webb County Sheriff's Department, Laredo, Texas.)

shrine may contain her crown with nine charms, including a hoe, pick, gourd, lightning bolt, scythe, shovel, rake, axe and mattock (an agricultural tool).

Yemaya

Yemaya is syncretized with Our Lady of Regla (Regla is a province in Cuba). This Orisha is considered to be the mother over the Orishas. Her name means "our mother whose children are the fish." Yemaya rules over seas and will be found in the form of seashells, mermaids, boats and other water-based items. Yemaya's colors are white and blue (Figure 4.4).

Babalu-Aye

This Orisha is syncretized with Saint Lazarus. Babalu-Aye is a title that means *father.* Babalu-Aye is a special Orisha to those who are dealing with sickness, as he owns the cure to sickness. He may also *cause* sickness. While he is historically associated with leprosy and smallpox, his contemporary association has also taken on AIDS as a sickness that he heals and causes. The shrines to Babalu-Aye may contain a pair of crutches as well as sackcloth. His shrine may also carry a beaded fly whisk known as the Aja. His color is purple.

Olokun

The Orisha Olokun is commonly called "Yemaya at the bottom of the ocean." The Orisha is a hermaphrodite being that is represented by an iron figure holding a sea snake and a mask. The artifacts of the Orisha Olokun are placed on the floor to mirror the bottom of the ocean.

Figure 4.4 The soperas of Yemaya and Oshun. These two Orishas are traditionally placed beside each other. Offerings of honey are placed in Oshun's presence to represent her sweet nature. Yemaya is flanked by seashells, mermaids and other items representing the ocean waters.

Orula/Orunmila

Orula is syncretized with Saint Francis of Assisi, and is the divine diviner. He owns the tools of divination that are used by the High Priest known as the Babalawo. He is represented by the divination tools called the Table of Ifa and the Okuele. His colors are green and yellow.

Osain

Osain is syncretized with Saint Raphael, and governs the forest and herbs. He is called upon to provide medicine for healing. Osain may be found in the form of a male figure with one arm, one leg and one ear. Osain is also depicted as a beaded gourd that may be decorated with feathers. His colors are the colors of all the Orishas.

The Ibejis

The Ibejis are the sacred twin Orishas. They are syncretized with Saint Cosme and Saint Damian. The Yoruba used these figures to represent the spirits of dead twins. In Santeria, the Ibejis are the sons of Chango. They will be found in the form of twin dolls or statues.

Aganyu

Aganyu is syncretized with Saint Christopher. He represents Earth forces, such as volcanoes and earthquakes. His shrines may contain depictions of a volcano. Aganyu is depicted in some myths as the father of Chango. His color is red.

Inle

Inle is syncretized with the archangel Raphael. Inle is the healer of the Orishas and is the patron of doctors and fishermen. Inle lost his tongue to Yemaya, so he must speak through the shells of Yemaya. A silver cross ornament is kept in his shrine to represent his presence. The cross has two snakes and two small fish hanging from its arms. The post of the cross has two snakes wrapped around it. Objects connected to fishing, such as a net and fishing line, may be found in his shrine. Inle is the owner of medicine. His colors are blue, yellow and white.

Oko

Oko is the owner the Earth and agriculture. He is represented by a miniature wagon and oxen. Oko will also be represented by a Spanish roof tile as his shrine.

There are literally hundreds of Orishas as well as many other significant characters of great importance to those who follow them. These spiritual "personalities" are popular among practitioners of Espiritismo (Spanish for "spiritualism").

One is El Negro Jose. Jose is used in the Orisha groups that use espiritismo. Jose is a statue of an elderly African man sitting in a chair. Sometimes he may be found leaning on a crooked staff. It is believed that spirits speak through his statue. He also may be used for spiritual protection.

Another spiritual figure that may be seen in statue form is known as La Madama. La Madama is depicted as an African woman wearing a dress, hoop earrings and a scarf on her head. Madama is a spiritual protector.

The Ancestors

Ancestor reverence in African religions has erroneously been labeled "ancestor worship" by many Western sources. World cultures including Asian, African, Indian and several others practice rituals and have sacred spaces devoted to the ancestors. These are not spaces where members "worship" ancestors, but areas that show a respect through aesthetics. In Santeria, the ancestors are called Eggun. The Eggun are recognized in the lives of devotees as being the spirits of the family members or members of the religious community who have died. The Eggun are recognized in rituals and in altars, and some Santeria practitioners will create a sacred space for the ancestors. The space is usually created in a dark place, such as a basement or bathroom. The space is marked off with chalk called Efun. Sacred marks are drawn on the ground and a staff is placed in the space. The staff is decorated with nine

Figure 4.5 Respect for dead ancestors is a concept found in many African traditional religions. Responders may observe the Boveda, the shrine for ancestral spirits. The shrine includes nine glasses of water representing spirits and a crucifix representing Jesus Christ and the head of the spirits.

colored ribbons with bells attached to the ribbons. Offerings of coffee and fruit may be placed in this space. The Eggun may be represented by a doll that is dressed in the colors of the ancestor's Orisha.

Many Santeria practitioners will have an altar called the Boveda. The Boveda is usually in the form of a table covered in a white cloth representing purity. There are nine glasses of water on the table surrounding a larger glass of water containing a crucifix. The Boveda is also decorated with flowers, photographs of the deceased and items related to the deceased. The Boveda is a sacred space and should not be touched or violated by nonpractitioners (Figure 4.5).

Group Structure

There are several branches of the religion known as Ramas throughout the United States. Ramas go by such names as La Pimienta, Culo Verde and Efunche. These traditions can be traced back to historical sources, and they have preserved specific practices and customs through the lineage.

The group structure in Santeria uses the traditional family as a model. Initiates become the children of the parental clergy. A new member who has not undergone any sort of initiation in Santeria is known in the community as Aleyo, which means *outsider.* Once a person has undergone initiation into the religion, he/she will be recognized first as a Santero (priest) or

Santera (priestess). The initiate is able to conduct rituals and access secret knowledge of spellwork and magic. They will also be referred to as a spiritual godchild known as Ahijado to the initiating priest or priestess. The godparent is then referred to as the Padrino (godfather) or Madrina (godmother) of the initiate.

Once the initiate has received the Orisha, they are recognized as being a Babalocha or Iyalocha. This title designates that the initiate is a priest or priestess of a specific Orisha.

The High Priest in Santeria is known as Babalawo, which means "father of the secrets." According to Santeria theology, only males can be Babalawos. The Babalawo can call upon Orun and perform divination. The Yoruba use a divination system known as Ifa; a very complex system of divination that takes years to learn. The Babalawo is considered a master of this type of divination.

The Babalawo uses a necklace called the Okuele. This chain is made of eight shells, palm nuts, bone and other materials. The chain is "thrown" onto a table or onto a mat on the floor and the Orishas speak through the pattern that the chain displays. There are 256 possible combinations of patterns called Letras, which are associated with a collection of proverbs. These proverbs contain advice on specific situations and, based on the proverb, the Babalawo may suggest an offering or rituals for a remedy.[4]

Rituals and Ceremonies

To understand the mechanics of the Santeria faith, it is important to know the various stages of initiation that members may attain.

Receiving the Necklaces

The first initiation ceremony is a Catholic baptism. However, the first initiation into the *Santeria* faith is performed strictly by a Santeria clergyman and known as "receiving the necklaces."

Called Elekes (*collares* in Spanish), the necklaces are sacred pieces of jewelry that put the initiate under the protection of the Orishas. The necklaces appear in different colors with varying numbers of beads on each strand. The color and number of beads refer to one of the many Orishas in the Santeria pantheon. The beads are typically 2-mm plastic beads that are strung on cotton cloth. The Santero, who performs a ritual over the necklaces, prepares the beads. The ritual gives the necklaces Ache, which transforms the beads from ordinary pieces of plastic into sacred symbols of power. The necklaces are washed in the sacred liquid known as Omiero (made from herbs, water [rain water, river water, ocean water, holy water] and steeped with a hot coal).

Figure 4.6 A Santero wearing the traditional white clothing and Elekes of the Santeria faith. Responders should avoid touching the sacred necklaces known as Elekes. If necessary, ask the patient to remove them.

The believer receives the necklaces as a means of spiritual protection. The wearing of these beads publicly identifies the initiate as being dedicated to the Orishas. The believer will initially receive the necklaces of Obatala, Chango, Oshun, Yemaya and Elegua (Figure 4.6).

The most common versions of the Orishas' elekes are

Elegua: His necklace is made of black and red beads usually in combinations of three.

Yemaya: Her colors are white and blue and are usually in combinations of seven.

Ogun: His colors are green and black. Many times a translucent green bead is used to indicate the initiate has "received the knife" of Ogun. The pattern is usually in seven or three.

Chango: His colors are red and white and are found in combinations of six.

Orula: His colors are green and yellow and most often arranged in patterns of one.

Oshun: Her colors are yellow and white and are found in combinations of five.

Babalu-Aye: His colors are purple and white.

The necklaces are treated with respect and are not to be worn while drinking alcohol or during sexual relations. If the necklace breaks apart, this is a sign that the Orisha has blocked something negative from happening to the initiate.

Practitioners may also receive a special beaded bracelet known as the Mano de Orula or Hand of Orula. This green and yellow bracelet is given by a Babalawo and is said to protect the owner from death (Iku).

Warriors

After an initiate has received the necklaces, the next step of initiation is to gain the protection of the Warriors, also known as Los Guerreros. This is a group of Orishas (Elegua, Ochosi, Ogun and Osun) that defend the initiate.

In Santeria myths known as Patakis, these gods travel together and the artifacts representing the Orishas are presented to the initiate in a ceremony. **Elegua** is presented in the form of a cement head with cowrie shells for facial features. **Ogun** is the Orisha governing iron. He is given to the initiate in the form of an iron cauldron. **Ochosi** is presented in the form of a metal crossbow. And, finally, **Osun** is given to the new initiate in the form of a metal chalice adorned with bells and a small metal rooster on its lid. Responders will see Osun placed near the doorway of a home and preferably at a high location. This allows Osun to watch out for danger. If the tool of Osun falls over, this means danger is coming. The chalice of Osun contains a hidden compartment that can be accessed by twisting the top of the chalice. The compartment contains powdered eggshell (Cascarila), stones, herbs and other items.

Receiving the warriors gives the initiate the spiritual protection of these Orishas. The warriors are kept inside the initiate's house and are to be "fed" offerings and sacrifices on a regular basis. Elegua is the first to be fed because he is the Orisha that opens the doorway to the spiritual realm. If Elegua is not fed first, the other Orishas may not be able to receive their offerings. Cold water is dripped onto his image to call his spirit. The priest who has presented the warriors to the initiate will perform a ritual in which a rooster is sacrificed in front of the warriors and then the deities are invited into the house in which they will reside. This ceremony is known as Ebbo de Entrada.

Cofa

Santeria teaches that man is guarded by a particular Orisha. This is similar to the concept of having a guardian angel. The Orisha is determined by a ceremony known as Cofa. The Orisha that is determined to be the personal guardian of the initiate is known as "owning the head." It is only after this determination is made can the Orisha be "crowned" onto the individual in the ceremony known as Ocha.

Kariocha

The major ceremony in which the initiate receives the personal protection of an Orisha is called Kariocha, which is a Lucumi word that means "put the Ocha on the head." This ceremony is also known as "making the saint." The ritual consists of the guardian Orisha being "crowned" onto the head of the initiate.

Kariocha leads the initiate through a spiritual rebirth. The initiate is given the tools to interact with the Orishas: the stones (Otans), the shells (Manos) and the tools (Herramintes) are placed inside ceramic vessels (Soperas).

During the ceremony (which can be very tedious), the initiate's head is cut open to receive the Orishas, along with the tools of the Orishas. The tools are placed above the head of the initiate inside the Sopera while songs are sung in the Lucumi tongue. (Trance possession can occur during this section of the rite.) The initiate's head is painted with symbols of the Orishas and an animal is rubbed over the body of the initiate and then sacrificed. The animal sacrificed differs according to the Orisha; for example, a rooster may be given for a child of Elegua.

The initiate then is taken to a river to be introduced and bathed by Oshun, the goddess of the river. The initiate removes his/her clothes and is bathed with the river water. Offerings are placed in the river, such as flowers, food and honey. Oshun takes the items to heaven to announce the birth of a new initiate. The initiate reaches into the river and retrieves a stone. (This sacred stone is seen as a home to the spirits. The myths of the Yoruba say that the Orishas descend to Earth in raindrops that fall into the river and land on stones. These stones are considered receptacles of spiritual power.) The stone is placed into a pot where it will act as a bridge between the Orishas and the initiate.

The ritual is a very complex ceremony that ends in a rite called the Asiento. The Asiento is the actual "seating" of the Orisha into the initiate. During this ritual is when the head of the initiate is cut with a small blade. The cut has several herbs applied to it to "crown" the essence of the Orisha into the head of the initiate. The initiate's head (Ori) is fed the blood of an animal as well as other ingredients, such as cocoa butter and coconut. The Orisha is then "seated" in the initiate's head.

The following day is known as the Middle Day. The initiate sits and eats lunch at a table prepared for him. After the lunch, the initiate is dressed in an outfit that contains the colors of the Orisha that he has received. A drumming ceremony follows in which the initiate is presented to the Santeria community.

The day after Middle Day is known as the Day of Ita. Ita is a reading performed by a gifted diviner. The diviner gives the initiate a list of taboos and a reading regarding the spiritual mother or father of the initiate. The details of this ceremony are recorded in a book known as the *Liberta*. This book is later given to the initiate after the completed initiation process.

Figure 4.7 The Sopera contains the "secrets" of the Orishas. The sacred stone, known as the Otan, is kept inside these vessels.

The initiate is dressed in white and must wear this color for a year. His head must remain covered and there are several restrictions placed on him. Restrictions involving sexual activity, diet and interaction with outsiders are usually listed in these taboos.

After three months, a sacrifice known as Ebbo Meta (or Three Month Ebbo) is performed. The initiate's hair is cut for the first time since the initiation.

The secrets of the Orishas are placed in Soperas, typically ceramic or wooden bowls that will be colored in a specific color that designates an Orisha (Figure 4.7). These bowls are kept in the homes of practitioners. The stone inside is routinely bathed in water and herbs. Animals may be sacrificed and the blood of the animal poured upon the stones. These are sacred objects and are treated as if the gods themselves were sitting in the bowls. The Soperas may be kept in wooden cabinets called Canastilleros.

At this point, the initiate becomes known as Omo Orisha or Child of the Orisha.

Obi

In order to communicate with the Orishas, Santeria practitioners use a tool known as an Obi. Use of the Obi is known as Darle Coco al Santo, which means "give coconut to the saint." Four pieces of coconut are "thrown" and the Orishas speak through the pattern in which the pieces land. There are five possible combinations in which the shells may land (Figure 4.8 and Figure 4.9).

There are five possible patterns in which the shells can fall.

Figure 4.8 The Orishas speak to practitioners through the coconut shells known as the Obi.

Figure 4.9 The coconut shells (Obi) are "thrown" after the Orisha is given three drops of water.

1. All white sides up—Alafia. This means a positive "yes."
2. All brown sides up—Oyekun. This means "no" and possibly death.
3. Three white sides and one brown side up—Itagua. This is an uncertain answer and the rinds are thrown again.
4. Two white sides up and two brown sides up—Ellife. This means a definite "yes."
5. Three brown sides up and one white side up—Okana Sode. This means "no," but may also mean death.

Diloggun

Another form of communication that is used to interact with the Orishas is the Diloggun, which is a system of divination that uses 16 cowrie shells as a means of hearing the gods. These shells are given to the initiate when he/she receives the otanes and soperas. The cowries, known as Caracoles, are "thrown" and land in various patterns. (The open side of the shell is the mouth of the Orisha.) The patterns are then interpreted by matching the particular pattern with a pattern known as the Odu. Initiates are traditionally trained by a divination specialist called the Italero.

Patakis

Believers are also taught about the Orishas and how to serve them through stories called Patakis. These are legends about the personalities and adventures of the Orishas. These stories instruct the believers on the specific powers Orishas can exert.

Offerings and Sacrifices

The practice of Santeria requires adherents to utilize the concept of offerings and sacrifices in interacting with the Orishas. The Orishas require minor offerings that are known as Adimu and sacrifices known as Ebbo. The Orishas may ask for sacrifices as a form of exchange in order to carry out requests (Figure 4.10).

Addimu

Addimus are small offerings to the Orishas. These can be foods, candles, candy and other materials. They are usually found on plates and in bowls in front the objects that represent Orishas.

Elegua is given corn meal with palm oil known as Manteca de Corojo, okra, coconuts, smoked fish (known as Eya), a bush rat (known as Jutia), toasted corn and candy.

Figure 4.10 An example of offerings to the Orishas.

Ogun is given green plantains and the gifts that Elegua requests. The sapodilla fruit is his favorite food.
Obatala is given eggwhites beaten with sugar as well as rice and vanilla puddings, milk and other white foods.
Chango is given a dish of okra and cornmeal cooked together, along with red apples and green bananas in groups of six.
Yemaya is given sweet plantains and pork rinds. Shrimp, dried coconut, white pears and okra are also found in her Addimu.
Oshun is given pumpkin, shrimp, eggs, spices, and raw fish. Honey is usually poured over the Addimu.
Oya is given eggplants and okra with cornmeal.
Babalu-aye is given cigars and the drink *aguardiente*. He also likes coconut butter, milk and bread.
Inle is given sweet wine and cake.

Ebbo

Perhaps the most misunderstood aspect of Santeria is the practice of animal sacrifice. This is known as Ebbo. The Ebbo is a sacrifice that gives the Orisha the energy found in the animal in exchange for the energy of the Orisha known as Ache. The blood that is given is called Eje.

There are particular stipulations that are followed in order to offer a sacrifice. The initiate that gives an Ebbo must first receive the knife used in the sacrifice in a ceremony called the Pinaldo. The knife is said to belong to the

Orisha Ogun. In fact, the ceremonial sacrifice is blamed on Ogun. The animal's blood is usually dripped onto the stones or tools that represent the Orisha. A prayer known as the Moyuba is spoken in the native Lucumi tongue.

The meat of the animals that are sacrificed is cleaned, cooked and eaten by the participants of the ritual. There is a saying, *La Sangre para El Santo, la carne para el Santero*, which translates: Blood for the saint, meat for the Santero. However, animals that are used to remove sickness or curses may not be eaten.

Each Orisha has a particular animal that is to be sacrificed for him or her.

Elegua is fed rum, cigars, turtles, goats, roosters and opossum.
Chango is offered goats, turtles, quail, roosters and rams.
Babalu-Aye is fed goats, roosters and pigeons.
Oshun prefers yellow hens and female goats.
Ogun is fed opossum, roosters, goats, pigeons and sometimes dogs.
Yemaya is given ducks, turtles, rams and roosters.
Oya is fed female goats, pigeons, hens and any black animals.
Aggayu is fed castrated goats, guinea hens and pigeons.
Obatala is fed female goats, hens, doves and guinea fowl.

Trance Possession

Responders that encounter certain Santeria ceremonies may witness a cultural phenomenon known as "trance possession." Trance possession is a practice observed by many world religions, and involves a practitioner opening him or herself up to a spiritual presence, such as a god or a spirit. The consciousness of the practitioner is taken over by the spirit allowing the spirit to use the practitioner as a conduit to communicate with the physical world. In this state, practitioners may espouse wisdom from the gods or even perform miracles. Scientific explanations of this activity say that this "altered state" of consciousness is a result of deep hypnosis from the drumming and singing that accompanies the ritual. One medical explanation has alleged that repeated auditory stimuli, such as drumming, can affect the central nervous system and the right hemisphere of the brain.

In Santeria, the possession of humans by the Orishas is described as *Subirse el Santo a su caballo*, translated as: "The saint climbs upon his horse." The presence of the Orisha at a ceremony is evidence that the Orisha has been pleased with the ceremony.

I have personally been told some very powerful stories about trance possession during Santeria ceremonies. One young lady shared her testimony of how she was healed of a brain tumor during an act of possession. Some stories tell of details of the Orishas using people to perform miraculous acts, such as eating and drinking hot food and liquids without being burned. Responders should understand that although trance possession may appear very "deviant" to outsiders, it is very much a part of the Santeria culture.

Responders that encounter scenes involving possession should be advised that these situations should be carefully approached. Signs that possession is occurring include:

- The presence of drumming, chanting and singing.
- The presence of a crowd of practitioners surrounding a single practitioner. Practitioners dressed in colorful clothing and handling large artifacts of the Orishas.
- During the possession by Ogun, the practitioner may swing a machete around to depict his character.
- Practitioners dancing or shaking in erratic manners. Possession may appear as a choreographed dance or violent rolling around on the floor. Possession by Elegua appears in the form of a dance in which the Orisha causes the practitioner to stand on one foot and twirl around.
- Display of supernatural acts, including consumption and handling of hot foods and substances.
- Increase in intensity of drumming and singing. This is to "call down" the Orisha.

Responders should not touch a practitioner exhibiting signs of trance possession. To touch the practitioner during possession can be viewed as interfering with the gods and can result in reactive behavior.

Most likely the ritual would be stopped due to the presence of outsiders. However, if you discover that you need to interact with someone at the scene of this ritualistic activity, it is advised that you address the leadership of the group. There is a culturally acceptable technique for the leadership to stop the act of possession without the responder violating a cultural taboo.

Espiritismo

A number of Santeria practitioners use a system of practices commonly referred to as Spiritism or, in the Latin American community, as Espiritismo. The practices are derived from the works of a nineteenth century French educator named Hippolyte Rivail, who is known by his pseudonym, Allan Kardec. Kardec organized a number of metaphysical practices that involved techniques to communicate with the dead. He popularized practices, such as spirit channeling and table tipping. Kardec's book, *The Spirit's Book,* features a number of questions regarding the work of spirits. The book is usually sold in Botanicas (retail stores that sell folk medicine, religious candles and statuary, amulets and other products regarded as magical) and supply stores for the Santeria faith. Practitioners may leave Kardec's books on their Boveda. Spiritism became an additional practice of Santeria when it caught on in areas such as Cuba and Puerto Rico.

Espiritismo uses doctrines and teachings of Christian and Spiritualist texts and combines elements of African and Latin indigenous teachings. Teachings usually claim that there is one creator God and several spirits created by God. The practice also teaches that the soul survives after death. After several stages of reincarnation, the soul may become a saint. Some spirits are known as Causas, which may cause problems in the lives of the living. Each person has several guardian spirits. Practitioners hold séances known as Sesion Espiritista in which the spirits of the dead may appear. The séance is held at a table covered in a white tablecloth known as the Mesa Blanca. White candles, white flowers and a bowl of water are placed on the table. The bowl of water is used to capture negative energies, which may manifest as bubbles in the bowl.

A practitioner may fall into a trance and become possessed by the spirit of the dead. Practitioners known as "mediums" act as channels for the spirits. There are a number of mediums, including those who can see spirits, hear spirits and see the future. Prayers from Kardec's books are read. Spirits of different cultures may also manifest themselves. Spirits known as Madamas, who are West African women; Gitanas, who are gypsies; Indios, who are Indians; Piratas, who are pirates; and Congos, who are Africans can appear. Spiritual masses, known as Misa Espiritual, are conducted by Santeria clergy.

Responders who encounter Espiritism rituals may observe trance possession and should avoid physical contact during acts of possession. This may appear to practitioners as an offense toward the spirits if the possessed are touched. Responders should address the leadership of the group to assist them in ending the session.

The medium may use the highly flammable "Florida Water" cologne to cleanse him or herself of negative energies.

Brujeria

The term *Brujeria* refers to the malevolent use of traditional tools of Santeria. This spell is known as a Trabajo, which means *work*. Dolls may be used to represent the victim of harmful magic. The Orishas may be called upon to perform horrendous acts on the enemies of practitioners. Dead animals may be left in front of the home of the intended victim. Responders may discover people who feel that they have been victims of Brujeria.

Holy Days

There are several different types of ceremonies performed in the Santeria community. One of the most popular is a celebration called the Bembe. Bembe means *party* in the Lucumi language. It is usually a drumming festival held in honor of Orishas. The ceremony may also be called a Tambor, which is a Spanish word denoting the fact that drumming ceremonies may be used in ceremonies. The days of celebration coincide with Catholic saints' days.

Following is a list of Orishas and their celebration days:

Orisha	Catholic Saint	Feast Day
Elegua	Saint Anthony	June 13
Orula	San Francisco Assisi	October 4
Obatala	Virgin de las Mercedes	September 24
Chango	Saint Barbara	December 4
Ogun	Saint Peter	June 29
Ochosi	Saint Norbert	June 6
Babalu-Aye	Saint Lazarus	December 17
Yemaya	Virgin de la Regla	September 7
Oshun	La Caridad del Cobre	September 8
Oya	Saint Teresa	February 2
Ibeji	Saint Cosmo and Damien	September 26
Inle	Saint Rafael	September 29

The drums used in the Bembe are sacred objects that are believed to contain spirits. The drums, known as the Bata, are three double-headed hourglass drums, and are consecrated and given a spirit known as Ana. Animals and offerings are presented to the drums. Drummers play a specific "call" in order to invite the Orishas to manifest by possessing a believer. A Bembe ceremony, known as Wemilere, is a ceremony using consecrated Bata drums.

One room used during the Bembe usually holds the throne of the Orisha. This room is often decorated in colorful banners and cloths spread across the walls and ceilings. There is also a tureen that holds the Orisha inside on the throne. If the celebration is an Asiento for the initiate, the Iyawo will be found sitting on the throne. There is a large offering of cakes and other items usually in the color of the Orisha. This is known as the Plaza. There are also fruit and vegetable offerings to the Orisha found on the floor. A basket filled with money, called the Derecho, is usually amidst the offering and is used to help pay for all the food, tools and time put into the celebration. At the base of the basket is a straw mat that visitors must fall down upon and show respect to the Orisha. A maraca or a bell is used to rattle or ring to call the Orisha.

The birthday of the initiate is celebrated every year. A celebration is held to commemorate the day that the initiate received the Orisha. Deserts, food and drinks are given to the Orisha, and shrines are built to display the objects and tureens of the Orisha.

Itutu

When a Santero dies, an elaborate ceremony called the Itutu is performed. This ceremony, performed by the community Santeros, takes one year to complete. The deceased is dressed in the clothing that belongs to his guardian Orisha. The tools of the Santero are broken apart and placed where the Orishas dictate.

Sacred Spaces

The sacred spaces used in Santeria typically include the tureens that house the Orishas as well as the numerous artifacts that are their tools. Responders may see the colorful tureens covered in cloths and beads throughout the residence of a Santeria practitioner. The shelves of a bookcase or dining room table may be decorated with the objects of the Orishas. Some homes will keep the warriors behind the doorway of the home for protection.

There are some objects that may be hung in the home, such as the talisman of Osain and the crossbow of Ochosi. Responders should note the presence of these items so as not to accidentally bump into them while responding to the scene.

Healing and Sickness

There are a number of cultural explanations as to the source of illness. The explanation is that the sickness is a punishment from God. The second cause of sickness is a punishment from the Orishas. Disobedience to an Orisha can become a cause of illness; someone using Brujeria against a patient can be the cause of sickness; lack of Ache can cause sickness; and, finally, the spirits of the dead (Eggun) also can cause health problems.

For healing, Santeria practitioners may consult the local Botanica, which serves as a supply shop for herbs and religious supplies. Santeros in the local community may also be consulted, and they may use divination to diagnose the illness.

Practitioners can suffer injury from disobeying the Orishas as well. Some of the divine punishments from the Orishas include:

Aganyu: Breaking neck, crushing body
Elegua: Misfortune, accidents
Inle: Madness
Obatala: Paralysis
Ogun: Problems with links, accidents involving iron
Olokun: Drowning, respiratory problems
Orula: Madness
Osain: Nervous system problems
Oshun: Problem with genitals and womb
Babaluaye: Skin infections
Chango: Accidents with fire, eyesight problems
Yemaya: Problems with the intestine

Responders may discover that practitioners have several cultural terms for illnesses. Understanding these terms can assist responders in attending to the needs of practitioners. Some of the more common terms used to describe illnesses are

Aro Otonowa — sickness from the sky
Aro Elese Olodumare — sickness from the hands of God
Aro Else Ocha — debt to santo that has to be repaid
Aro Elese Eleda — sick because of disobedience

Methods of Healing

There are several remedies used in Santeria to heal illnesses. One of the most common forms of healing involves a "head cleansing." The head, known as Ori, is considered the location of the soul and of the Orisha in an initiate. The Rogacion de Cabeza is a ritual cleansing that involves the Santero using a number of elements to cleanse the head. Grated coconut, powdered eggshell, cotton, and cocoa butter are made into a paste. These items represent Obatala, the father of purity. The items are placed on the head, neck, arms, knees and feet of the patient. Prayers are spoken to ask for cleansing. A coconut is broken and is used in the paste and the other portion is kept to use in divination. The patient's head is covered in the paste and wrapped in white cloth. The patient sleeps overnight with the wrap intact. The Santero uses the coconut to ask the Orishas if the cleansing is acceptable.

The Elekes may need to be refreshed in order to provide Ache. The necklaces are soaked in an herb liquid known as Omiero (see Santeria Herbalism) or in a glass of water.

The Santero may prescribe magical baths, which contain perfumes, flowers, cascarilla and holy water, for the patient to receive spiritual strength. The patient may also need to receive artifacts like the Elekes or the Warriors.

Santeria Herbalism

Herbs play a major part in many African religious traditions. Santeria is no exception. The power of herbs is said to have come from the forest that is home to the medicines used by the indigenous healers of Africa and the New World healers of Santeria. While herbs and the healing power of the Orishas are powerful in the lives of believers, most practitioners do not refuse the assistance of Western medicine in healing. However, there are some spiritual issues that can only be solved by the Orishas and magical herb work.

The word Ewe is the Yoruba word used to describe herbs, plants and trees. The herbs contain Ache and are used in fresh and dried forms. (Fresh green herbs are said to hold more Ache.) Herbs are usually purchased from local Botanicas where there is at least one person who is an expert in herbs. Each Ewe belongs to a specific Orisha. It is in concert with these Orishas that the herbs have the most power.

The Orisha Osain is the "lord" over herbal work. In Santeria mythology, Osain is a one-legged, one-armed, one-eyed being. He is called upon to give the power of herbal magic to practitioners.

Some Santeria practitioners are said to be born with the "gift of Osain," which means that they are natural born herbalists. Responders may discover an artifact known as the Talisman of Osain hanging in or near the homes of practitioners. The talisman is a gourd or round clay vessel that is filled with various materials, including animal blood, herbs, water and other ingredients. The talisman may have a feather hanging from it or it may be decorated in numerous colored beads. The talisman gives the owner the powers of herbal magic from Osain and can guide them in spellwork.

Herbs are used in the healing rites known as Despojos and may be bundled and passed over the body to remove sickness and bring positive energy. Herbs can be placed in bathwater to create healing.

The responder may discover jars or bottles filled with murky appearing liquids. The Omiero is a liquid that is sacred to the Santeria faith, and is composed of twenty-one herbs, rum, palm oil, powdered eggshell, honey, pepper, kola nuts and the blood of animals. It is used to "refresh" the Elekes (necklaces) and the Otanes (stones).

Some of the common herbal remedies used in Santeria include:

Folk Name	Botanical Name
Albahaca *Used to remove headaches; may be crushed to stop stomachaches or made into a tea*	Basil
Alcanfor *Used to remove evil*	Camphor
Anise *Tea made from anise relaxes and eliminates fatigue*	Anise seed
Atipola *Used to foretell the future*	Hogweed
Espartillo *Used to protect against evil*	Sporobolus
Manzanilla *Good for the stomach as well as a sedative*	Chamomile
Maravilla *A natural astringent used to make a tea that cures colic*	Witch hazel
Mejorana *Used as a tea to ease labor pains*	Marjoram
Rompe Saraguey *Used against evil*	Siam weed
Yerba Buena *Cleanses bad skin*	Spearmint

Some plants that are used in healing include:

Escoba Amarga belongs to San Lazaro, healer of skin diseases. The plant is used in a bath to heal skin problems.
Obatala owns white cotton bush. Seeds help asthma.
Alamo, sassafras, yerba mora are used to treat sorcery.
Mustuerzo is used for kidney problems and in head cleansing.
Sabila is used to treat vaginal inflammations.

Plants also may be used to fight witchcraft. The plant Abre Camino (*Trichilia havanesis*) is used to remove the source of witchcraft. Petals of the Galan de Dia (*Cestrum Diurnum*) are spread throughout a house to keep away witchcraft. Pieces of Ruda (*Ruta Chalepensis*) are placed by doorways to protect the home.

Mercury

The ritualistic use of the chemical mercury in Santeria and other Voudon religions is a common practice. Mercury, known as Azogue, is used in a number of magical operations. The chemical is known to ward off spirits, speed up spirits and attract money and love.

In 1999, the United States Environmental Protection Agency (EPA) formed a multiagency task force to study the ritualistic use of mercury in various folk traditions. The task force discovered that a number of Botanicas sold the substance to customers in the Santeria, Palo, Voodoo and Espiritismo communities. Mercury was discovered to be placed in small capsules for amulets. Mercury was also used in baths and sprinkled around homes of practitioners.[6]

Short-term exposure to mercury can affect the respiratory system and result in pneumonitis, severe bronchiolitis, pulmonary edema and/or death. Long-term exposure to small doses of mercury results in neurological problems.

Articles of Comfort

Responders assisting members of the Santeria religion will discover a number of material artifacts used to provide protection and spiritual comfort. The most visible object is the Elekes, the sacred necklaces received in the first initiation. There are a number of these objects that practitioners may have in their possession.

Idé

The Idé is a bracelet that represents the Orisha Orula. The bracelet is composed of yellow and green beads, and represents the protection that is provided by Orula. Orula is believed to have wrestled with the spirit of death known as Iku. Iku promised Orula that if she identifies her followers with a sign death will not take them before their time. The bracelet is the symbol that protects the wearer from death. It is traditionally worn on the left wrist.

Macuto

The Macuto is an amulet that has been prepared by a priest or priestess. The amulet is a small packet that is covered in colored beads and a cowrie shell. The amulet can be prepared to serve a variety of purposes. Some amulets will give their owner strength, peace or financial success. The Macuto is usually kept in the pocket of the practitioner.

Figure 4.11 A priestess conducts a ceremony for the Orishas. If responders arrive during ceremonies, it is recommended that they address the leadership if possible. This will assist in halting ritualistic activities in order to assist the patient.

Responder Issues

Responders that encounter Santeria rituals should address the leadership of the group and demonstrate respect and professionalism to all participants (Figure 4.11).

There are a number of objects in Santeria that are considered spiritually empowered. Responders should avoid opening the soperas and shrines of the Orishas.

Responders may encounter initiates wearing the elekes. The patient should be allowed to wear the necklaces as they provide a source of spiritual comfort to the practitioner. However, if a responder must remove the beads in order to give proper treatment, if possible they should ask the practitioner to remove the beads.

Responders may discover lacerations on the head of initiates from some of the various rituals. There are many religious "secrets" in the religion of

Figure 4.12 Responders should use caution if handling ritual objects during an investigation. Animal blood may be present on the tools that have been ritually "fed."

Santeria. Be advised that you may have to be tactful in inquiring about scars and marks acquired during rituals.

Responders should use caution when handling artifacts, such as amulets. Residue of mercury may be present among these objects. If mercury is present, stay upwind from the area of contamination. Use a mercury spill kit if needed and utilize self-contained breathing apparatus (SCBA) if possible.

Responders handling artifacts and or patients may discover the presence of animal blood from sacrificial rituals (Figure 4.12). Utilize gloves, masks and eye protection as needed.

Responders who may be removing ritual objects, such as drums, should be advised that animal skins can be used for drum heads. Diseases may be present in these skins. Use protective clothing to avoid contamination.

Some offerings include the use of guinea pepper. Practitioners may chew on the pepper before offering the seeds. These may cause slight irritation in the practitioner's mouth.

Syncretic religions such as Santeria have changed historically and evolved from their origins in Africa. In the same theme, the approaches and tactics used by healthcare professionals when interacting with people of various religious faiths should change and evolve with the needs of the client culture.

References

1. American Religious Identification Survey 2001, The Graduate Center of the City University of New York, Web site at: http://www.gc.cuny.edu/faculty/research_studies/aris.pdf
2. O'Brien, David M., *Animal Sacrifice and Religious Freedom: Church of the Lukumi Babalu-Aye v. City of Hialeah*, 2004, Lawrence: University of Kansas Press, 10.
3. Brown, David, *Santeria Enthroned*, Chicago: University of Chicago Press, 2003.
4. Bascom, William, *Sixteen Cowries: Yoruba Divination from Africa to the New World*, Bloomington: Indiana University Press, 1980.
5. Gonzalez Wippler, Migen, *Santeria: The Religion*, Original Publications, 1989.
6. Task Force on Ritualistic Uses of Mercury Report, United States Environmental Protection Agency, Office of Emergency and Remedial Response, Washington, D.C.: OSWER 9285.4-07, EPA/540-R-01-005, December 2002.

Palo and Kongo Religions

5

Assessing the Scene

> You receive a call that police are on the scene of an incident in which they have arrested members of a group on charges of grave robbing. Officers are reporting that a member of the group is covered in blood and in need of medical attention in a residential home. Upon arriving, an officer leads you into the basement of the house where the police are crowded around a man sitting on the floor covered in blood. The walls are also covered in blood and display strange drawings of symbols, and the room is filled with iron pots containing numerous sticks. A human skeleton sits in a chair in the back of the room.

There is very little information available to the public in the United States about the Kongo religions. The majority of the literature available on the subject is written in Spanish and is from Cuba where the religion is openly practiced. Because of the secretive nature of Palo Mayombe (usually referred to simply as Palo) and other Bakongo religious traditions, responders may rarely see the religious artifacts of these religions. Rites are practiced in secret to preserve their sacred customs and because of the controversial use of human remains in their practices. (The word *Kongo* is commonly used by religious historians to refer to the kingdom of the Bakongo people. The spelling is considered "traditional" as opposed to *Congo*, which refers to the new political state in the region.)

Bantu Traditions

Las Reglas de Congo is a term used to refer to the numerous religious traditions of the Bantu people of Central Africa. These traditions include a number of religious cultures that are seen in the United States. These traditions or "branches" are known as Ramas. Each tradition has its own unique practices, symbols and social structures. Some of the Bantu religious traditions include Brilumba, Kimbisa, Corta Lima and Palo Mayombe.[1] Palo Mayombe is the Bantu religion that appears to be the most widely practiced throughout the United States.

In order to understand the modern day practice of Palo Mayombe, it is important for responders to understand the basic elements of the Central African Bantu religion.

Bantu Religious Elements

Bantu religions teach that the world is divided between that of the living and that of the dead. Spirits of the dead and spirits of nature are believed to interact with humanity, and in order to properly interact with these spirits, the Bantu enlist the help of the local herbalist and healer. The Bantu ritual specialist is known as the Nganga. Through the use of medicines, known as Nkisi, the specialist could solve the problems of the local community. He/she would use elements found in nature, such as stones, bones, dirt and water to communicate with the world of the dead and with nature.[2]

The Bantu religions and their ritual specialists were spread throughout the world when many of the Bantu were driven into slavery. A large concentration of Bantu people (properly known as Bakongo) were taken to Cuba where their religions were suppressed by the colonialists. The religions started to take on different forms when the slaves began to incorporate European Christianity and the Yoruba traditions from Africa into their rites and practices.

The Nganga of Africa was transformed from being the name of a ritual specialist to the name for a ritual vessel. The contemporary version of the Nganga is a clay or iron vessel that houses the spirits of nature and of the dead (Figure 5.1). The Bantu religions were brought to the United States throughout the mid-twentieth century. While early members of these religions were

Figure 5.1 The Nganga is the central vessel used in Palo Mayombe and other assorted Kongo faiths. The Nganga contains the elements that form the Nkisi (or sacred medicines) used by the Bantu people groups of the Kongo.

predominantly Latinos, a number of Anglo Americans have become initiated throughout the years. Today, the Bantu religions operate in the United States, although somewhat secretly. The secrets of tradition and some of the practices of the religions make it difficult for them to be practiced in the same open manner that thet are in Cuba. It is for this reason that responders may have difficulty in openly communicating with practitioners of Bantu religions.

Beliefs and Practices

The primary tradition we will examine will be Palo Mayombe, as it is the most evident of the Bantu religions in the United States.

The fundamental teachings of Palo Mayombe is that the creator of the world is known as Nzambi, a benevolent being that has been compared by some practitioners to the Judeo–Christian concept of a creator god. In Kongo past culture, Nzambi was a benevolent creator that gave man medicines to help the world. These medicines were known as Minkisi.[3]

According to Kongo mythology, Nzambi gave man the instruction on how to create sacred medicines from plants. These medicines had to be infused with a spiritual power in order to be functional. This spiritual power was attained by taking dirt from graveyards. The soil from these areas contained the spiritual energy from the dead who were buried there.

Bantu belief teaches that the spirits of the dead (known as the Nfumbe) can interfere with the lives of the living (Figure 5.2). The dead can also be called upon to perform work for the living. The spirit of a dead human is

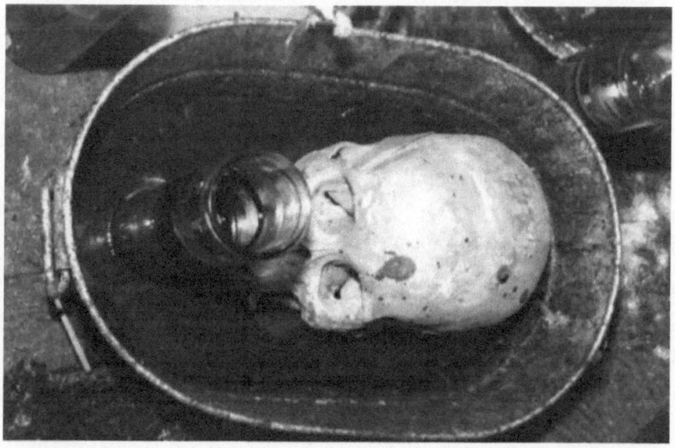

Figure 5.2 Human bones are components that are traditionally used in the Nganga to represent the Nfumbe or spirits of the dead. The skull, known as Kiyumba represents the intelligence of the dead. (Courtesy of Michael Vincent, Orange County Sheriff's Office Criminal Investigations, Orlando, Florida.)

placed inside the Nganga. The spirit becomes a servant to the ritual specialists who own the Nganga.

Alongside the dead, the spirits of nature (known as Mpungo) are placed in the Nganga. Mpungo also are found to be identified with Catholic saints. Practitioners may refer to the Mpungo by one of its several different names. The Spanish, Yoruba, Bantu or Catholic saint name may be used when speaking of the spirits.

Kadiempembe (also known as Lungombe) is the dark counterpart to the creator. Palo practitioners claim that magic can be performed with the power of the light (Nzambi) or the powers of darkness (Kadiempembe). Those who use magic for benevolent work are known as Palo Christianos, while those who use the adversarial powers are known as Palo Judios. Judios (or Jewish Palo) merely refers to the absence of Christian images and references in the ritual vessel. The traditional indicator that a Nganga may be used for Christian workings is the presence of a crucifix and holy water.

The myths and characteristics of the Mpungo dictate what responders will find in the Nganga. The Nganga will be decorated and filled with implements, colors and symbols that refer to the Mpungo. Once inside the vessel, these items are known as the Nkisi.

Some Palo houses use syncretism (the fusing of different religious beliefs) much like that found in Santeria. The saints of the Catholic Church and the Orishas of Santeria may be used to identify the Mpungo.

The following are some of the most popular Mpungo of Palo Mayombe:

Tiembla Tierra or Mama Kengue: Rules over the Earth. Associated with the Orisha Obatala and the Virgin de las Mercedes. The color white is used in the shrine to Tiembla Tierra. Represents wisdom and justice.

Mama Chola or Choya Wengue: Rules over the river. Associated with the Orisha Oshun and the saint The Virgin de la Caridad del Cobre. The color yellow is used in her shrines alongside items associated with the river. Represents richness and pleasures.

Siete Rayos or Mama Nsasi: Rules over thunder and fire. Associated with the Orisha Chango and Saint Barbara.

Kobayende or Tata Nfumbe: Rules over disease and healing. Known as King of the Dead. Associated with the Orisha Babalu-aye and Saint Lazarus.

Centelle Ndoki or Mariwanga: Rules over the cemeteries and owns the gate between life and death. Associated with the Orisha Oya and the Virgin de la Candelaria.

Gurufinda: Rules over the forest and herbal magic. Associated with the Orisha Osain and Saint Norbert.

Lucero: Rules over the crossroads of fate and opens doorways. Associated with the Orisha Eleggua and the Catholic Saint Anthony and Nino Atocha.

Kalunga or Madre De Agua: Rules over the ocean waters and fertility. Associated with the Orisha Yemaya and the Catholic saint Our Lady of Regla.

Zarabanda: Rules over strength, work and iron. Associated with the Orisha Ogun and Saint Peter.

There are a number of other spirits that can inhabit the Nganga. The Nfuri are wandering spirits, the Bakalu are ancestral spirits, and the Nkuyu are ancestors who are paying the debts for negative acts during their life. They are ghost-like beings that can haunt someone.

Nganga: The Cauldron

As noted above, the spirits of the dead and of nature are kept together in a vessel known as the Nganga. The Nganga is viewed much like a small universe that is composed of trees, rivers and mountains represented by dirt, water and tree branches. Tree branches, known as Palos, are placed in bundles of twenty-one into the Nganga cauldron, which is made of clay or iron. A special stone, known as Matari, is placed first in the pot and elements of water, shell, herbs and dirt are then added. The elements found in the Nganga will reflect the Mpungo to which the pot is dedicated. For example, a cauldron dedicated to a spirit of water may contain materials, such as boat oars, fish and fishnet. Other common elements include dirt from cemeteries, church grounds and jails.

Responders may discover a small piece of bamboo or cane that is sealed on both ends (Figure 5.3). This is the cana brava and it is most likely filled with mercury. The cana brava acts as a thermometer for the cauldron. The mercury can keep the spirits "cool."

Bones

Responders who encounter Palo Mayombe shrines may discover the presence of animal and human bones in the Nganga. Bones play a special part in the building of the Nganga as they represent the ancestors and the spirits of the dead. The energy of these spirits resides in the bones. It is by using these energies that the practitioners of Palo Mayombe can interact with the spirits of the dead. Practitioners refer to human bones as the Nfumbe.

The primary human bones used in the Nganga are the skull, tibia and femur. The skull, known as the Kiyumba, acts as the "intelligence" of the dead and as a conductor between the world of the dead and the world of the living. The skull is placed in the center of the Nganga's components. The tibia and femur may be found inside the Nganga or near the vessel. These bones can be used as scepters when conducting rituals. These are the primary bones

Figure 5.3 The cana brava is a piece of cane or bamboo that is filled with mercury and sealed off. Responders who are handling evidence from the Nganga should be cautioned in touching these objects. (Photo courtesy of Emily Owens, Hutchins Police Department, Hutchins, Texas.)

that are used; however, there are a number of case examples in which additional bones were found inside the Nganga. In some cases, the skullcap has been discovered being used as a "bowl" to hold various substances, such as herbs or water.

There are a number of sources that Palo practitioners use to obtain human bones, including medical specimen companies and scientific supply companies. In recent years bones from these sources have frequently been discovered to be the skeletal remains of Chinese males. There are currently a number of Internet Web sites that offer human bones. There also have been some Palo practitioners who have obtained bones by robbing graves.

The possession of human bones is a common practice for members of many African religious traditions. The bones are kept to show honor and respect for the dead. However, in the United States, state laws govern the sale, possession and transport of human bones. Nonlaw enforcement responders who encounter bones should contact law enforcement for assistance. Physical anthropologists should be contacted to identify the bones. The skull (or Kiyumba) can be used to identify such aspects as sex, race and age of the bones.

Sacred Spaces

Because of its powerful nature, the Nganga is kept in a private area. The vessels of Palo Mayombe will traditionally be found in a shed or small house,

Figure 5.4 The working space of a Palero is shown. The Nganga is traditionally kept in a secret location as it is a very powerful artifact that houses spirits considered dangerous and volatile. (Courtesy of Michael Vincent, Orange County Sheriff's Office Criminal Investigations, Orlando, Florida.)

called Nso Nganga. The shed can be a garage or a small building used for storage. Some cases have revealed the presence of the Nganga inside a bedroom closet (Figure 5.4).

Responders may see a number of symbols and cryptic signs painted on the floors and walls near the Nganga. These symbols are known as Firma, which are symbols and signatures that represent religious concepts in Palo, such as rituals, deities and prayers (Figure 5.5). The Firma are painted in white, black or red colors. The symbols most commonly used are crosses, Xs, circles, skulls and arrows. Each symbol represents a concept that is communicated to the spiritual world. Palo practitioners are taught the hidden meanings behind these symbols through oral teachings passed on by the priesthood.[4]

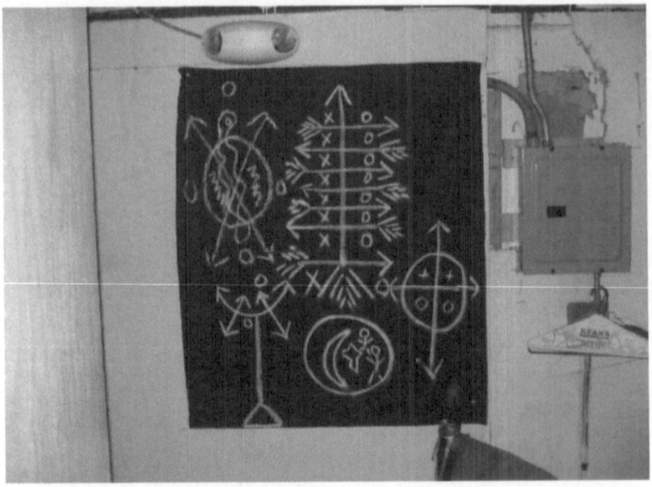

Figure 5.5 The Firma is a drawing that represents Bantu religious concepts, such as deities, rituals and the intention of practices. Responders may observe these images painted inside ritual spaces where Palo is practiced.

The sacred vessels and artifacts of Palo Mayombe may be discovered when responding to calls. Following are a few of the most common vessels and artifacts that are used in the practice of Palo Mayombe.

Lucero

The vessel for Lucero is very similar in appearance to the artifact of Eleggua in Santeria. Lucero is usually found in the form of a cement head decorated with cowrie shells or painted facial features. Lucero may be placed on a terra cotta plate or in a cauldron. His vessel may contain toys, candy or goats (Figure 5.6).

Siete Rayos

The Nganga to Siete Rayos may be painted red. The vessels associated with Siete Rayos may contain bones from birds, stones and red roosters. The skull and horns of a large ram is a favored item in his Nganga.

Zarabanda

The vessels for Zarabanda always contain elements made of iron and are always placed in an iron cauldron. The vessel can contain machetes, railroad spikes, knives and tools.

Mama Sholan

Mama Sholan is typically found in a ceramic or terra cotta pot. The vessel may contain fishnet, boat oars, river water and honey.

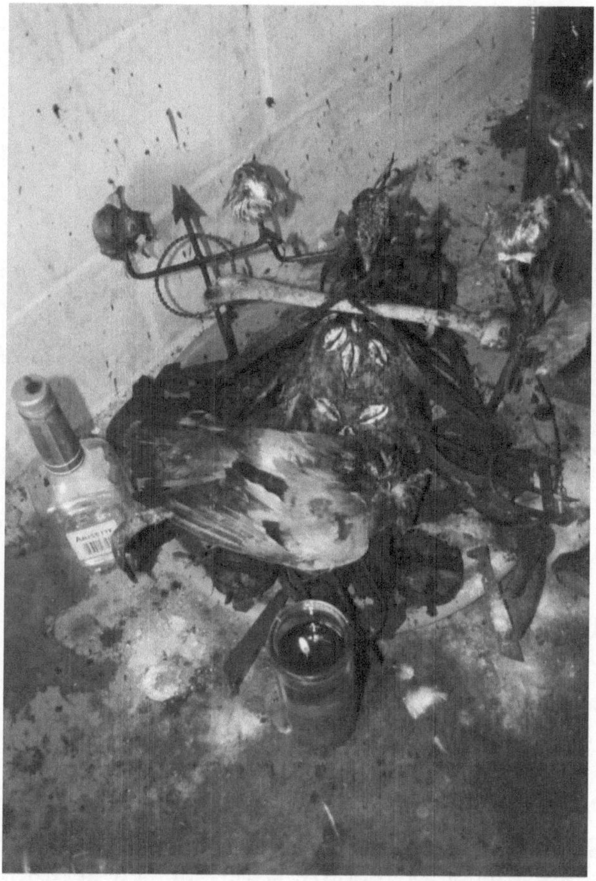

Figure 5.6 Responders may discover the presence of blood and remains of animals in the shrines of Palo practitioners. Blood is called Menga and is used as an offering to the deities. This is a Lucero that has been fed various birds. (Courtesy of Michael Vincent, Orange County Sheriff's Office Criminal Investigations, Orlando, Florida.)

Centelle Ndoki

The vessel for Centelle Ndoki may contain cat bones and cemetery dirt because she rules the cemetery, the dead and creatures of the night.

Tiembla Tierra

The vessel for Tiembla Tierra may be colored white. The vessel is fed white animals and may contain snakes and bird remains.

Figure 5.7 Francisco is a figure that represents deified African ancestors and is also used in shrines to represent the Mpungo Siete Rayos.

Madre de Agua

The vessel for Madre de Agua may contain elements related to water and the ocean because she rules the sea and all the riches that dwell in it. The vessel can contain remains from a ram and turtle.

Francisco and Francisca

These two figures are depicted in the form of an elderly African man and woman. They are used to symbolize strong deified ancestors in the religion. The hardships of slavery are depicted in the images of these two figures (Figure 5.7).

Seven Congos

This image is depicted as a female "mammy"-type figure with seven children sitting around her. These images represent the seven tribes of the Congo that landed in Cuba.

Group Structure

Organized Palo groups are known as Munanso, a group of worshippers dedicated to a particular deity. The name of the Munanso may reflect its affiliation. A group, such as Munanso Siete Rayos, reflects dedication to the Mpungo Siete Rayos. The initiated priest in Palo is known as the Palero. Palo is traditionally handed down through family lineage.

Members of the Munanso may hold a particular office in the temple. The Ngueyo is a practitioner who has made a pact with the Mpungo of his godfather. The Tata Nkisi is one who has acquired knowledge of using herbs and magic, but has not attained the Nganga. The Tata Nganga is a leader who has received the Nganga and can lead a Munanso. The Tata Ndibilinongo not only has an Nganga, but has spiritual godchildren. The highest level of initiation is the Tata Luwongo who is known as the godfather of the Prenda. The Bakonfula acts as an assistant to the Tata of the Munanso. Also known as the Mayombero, the Bakonfula assists with teaching new initiates about the symbols, rituals and courtesies of the temple.

Rituals and Ceremonies

There is a specific cultural etiquette that practitioners of Palo Mayombe must follow while interacting with the spirits of the Nganga. The practitioner addresses the spirits with a salutation of *Sala Maleko, Maleko Sala.*

The practitioner treats the spirits with respect, but will always hold a dominant role over the spirits. Some houses use a leather bullwhip (Kubula) to dominate the Nganga and show authority over the spirits while "whipping" them into obedience. Practitioners may burn piles of gunpowder called Fula to get the attention of the spirits. And traditional songs and prayers known as Mambos may be uttered to call upon the spirits.

Divination

Practitioners may use objects to interact with the spirits in the Nganga. The Chamalongo are four pieces of coconut that are thrown to the ground in front of the Nganga (Figure 5.8). The pattern in which the pieces land is interpreted by the practitioner as a response from the spiritual world. Cowrie shells, known as Encobo, are also used to interpret the will of the spirits.

An artifact, known as the Vititi Mensu, is an animal horn used in divination rites. The horn is filled with herbs and various materials and then capped off with a mirror and wax. The practitioner is trained to use the artifact to see messages from the spirits by looking into the mirror.

Sacrifices

Animal sacrifices in Palo Mayombe are performed using a knife called the Mbele. The Mbele must be received by an initiate from the Mpungo Zarabanda. The blood of animals is used to feed the spirits that live in the Nganga. Blood is known as Menga and is an essential tool in interacting with the deities. Blood is taken from various animals offered to the Nganga, including chickens, goats, rams, sheep and dogs. Exotic animals may be used as well: snakes, spiders and even horses.

Figure 5.8 The Chamalongos are used as a divination tool to communicate with the spirits inside the Nganga. The shells are thrown and the pattern in which they land is interpreted by the priest.

The animal is presented to the spirit as prayers (Mambos) are offered. The animal is killed and the blood of the animal is poured onto the objects inside the Nganga. The carcass of the animal is placed inside the cauldron where it will remain until the practitioner feels it is necessary to remove it (Figure 5.9).

Initiation

The Palo initiation begins with a pact between god (Nsambi), the living (Munanso) and the dead (Nfumbe). The initiate is given a ceremonial bath filled with sacred herbs and liquids (Figure 5.10).

The initiate may be taken to a cemetery to find the spirit that will work in the Nganga. The priest will perform divination over various graves in order to find a willing spirit. Rum is poured onto a grave and the priest listens for the sound of rumbling which signifies that the spirit inside is willing to work in the Nganga. Bones may be taken from the grave and placed in the pot alongside bits of soil. Water, animal bones, peppers and vegetables are added to create a new ritual vessel. Ingredients will also be taken from the priest's Nganga and placed in the new pot in order to "give birth" to the Nganga.

The initiate is blindfolded and a number of ritualistic cuts are made on his/her body. A razor or spur is used to cut the flesh in a number of locations. This cutting is known as the Rayado, initiates may refer to this as being "scratched in." The neck, feet, hands and chest area are cut and the blood of

Figure 5.9 This Nganga was discovered near the scene of a double homicide. Although the discovery of the cauldron coincided with the discovery of the crime scene, the vessel was found to be unrelated to the crime. (Photo courtesy of Emily Owens, Hutchins Police Department, Hutchins, Texas.)

the initiate is placed in the Nganga to bind him or her to the spirit. Gunpowder, rum and powdered bone can be placed in the cuts and then the cuts are sealed with wax.

A Firma of the spirit is carved into the flesh of the initiate. The initiate also receives a secret symbol that is known only to members of the Munanso.

Figure 5.10 The initiate stands on this firma to make the Pacto or "pact" with the dead (Nfumbe).

The tongue also may be cut. Drumming and chanting are performed to invoke the spirits, and Fula is burned to obtain messages from the spirits.

The initiate receives a large strand of beads called the Collar de Bandera. These are worn during certain Palo ceremonies. The bead's color reflects the Mpungo that the initiate serves. The strand of beads is about four feet in length and is worn from the left side of the body over to the right side.

Trance possession can occur during this ceremony. The possession in Palo allows the initiate to see with the eyes of the spirits. This "mounting" of the initiate by the spirit is known as Montado. The Priest will blow cigar smoke behind the ears of the initiate to bring about possession.

Herbalism

Herbs play a very important role in Palo Mayombe practices. The herbs of the forest contain the energies necessary to heal and protect mankind. One of the most important herbal mixtures in Palo Mayombe is called Chamba, which is a mixture of herbs, peppers, alcohol, bone and other ingredients. Chamba is used to purify ritual objects and to invigorate the spirits (Figure 5.11).

There are a number of special powders created in Palo Mayombe known as Mpolos. These powders are made from cemetery dirt, powdered bone, snake and bat skins. The branches of the silk cotton tree, known as the Ceiba, are used in various healing rites in Palo.

Figure 5.11 Shown are bottles of the substance Chamba, which is a liquid that is sprayed onto ritual vessels. The traditional Chamba recipe contains water, alcohol, peppers, herbs and various plants. Some recipes use powdered bone.

Some of the common herbs used in the Kongo traditions include:

Mecheiso: *Ocimum basilicum* (basil)
Dioke: *Ambrosia artemisiiflora*, Carbonero
Naona: *Cassia biflora*, Carbonero
Espanta Muerto: *Petiveria alliacea* (anamu)
Yunkagua: *Guaiacum officinalis* (lignum vitae tree)
Cereke: *Ficus nitida* (Indian laurel; bay laurel)
Inkita: *Amyris Balsamifera*, Palo Cuaba (West Indian Rosewood)

Articles of Comfort

Initiates may have received beaded necklaces known as Collar de Bandera (see section on Initiation above). These necklaces are nearly four-feet long and contain beads, shells and chain. They are worn over the left shoulder during ceremonies.

Charms known as Makutos or Resguardos are created by Paleros. These charms may be found in the form of bones wrapped in cloth. The color of the cloth may reflect the Mpungo to which the charm is dedicated.

The Mpaka is an artifact that is made from an animal horn. The horn includes ingredients found in the Nganga and is sealed with wax. The horn may be used to transport the fundamental materials used in the Nganga.

The Ceiba tree, which is a silk cotton tree, is considered sacred in the religion of Palo Mayombe. The Ceiba contains spirits of the dead. The branches of the Ceiba are used in healing medicines.

Healing and Sickness

The branches of various trees contain healing properties. To protect a child from evil, a branch from the Iroko tree is wrapped in red ribbon and hung above the crib.

A piece of jet (a form of fossilized wood), known as Azabache, is worn on a necklace or bracelet to protect against the evil eye.

Baths also are used to heal and the bath water is filled with colognes, herbs, flowers and trees branches.

Rogación de Cabeza is a head cleanser used to remove negative energies and vibrations.

Responder Issues

When encountering a group practicing its religious ceremonies, realize that it may be awkward for the group to be seen in ritual. Some members of the group may not be public about their faith or they may have encountered negative reactions to their faith in the past. Respond in a kind and professional manner.

Allow the patient to carry any necessary objects of protection that may give him or her comfort: amulets, jewelry, talismans, gemstones or any other items that may be of comfort to the patient.

Responders should use caution when handling artifacts, such as amulets. Residue of mercury may be present among these objects. If mercury is present, stay upwind from the area of contamination. Use a mercury spill kit if needed and utilize self-contained breathing apparatus (SCBA), if possible (Figure 5.12).

Responders may discover lacerations on the body of initiates from some of the various rituals. There are many religious "secrets" in the religion of Palo Mayombe. Be advised that you may have to be tactful in inquiring about scars and marks acquired during rituals. Also be advised that materials, such as human bone and gunpowder, may be placed in these cuts.

Responders handling artifacts and/or patients may discover the presence of animal blood from sacrificial rituals. Utilize gloves, masks and eye protection as needed.

If responders discover an Nganga, they should contact law enforcement, as the Nganga may contain human remains. The origins of these remains should be analyzed by a local medical examiner. Remains may have been

Figure 5.12 Responders should be aware that the use of mercury in a ritualistic vessel is quite common in Palo Mayombe. (Courtesy of Michael Vincent, Orange County Sheriff's Office Criminal Investigations, Orlando, Florida.)

attained by illegal means, such as illegal trafficking or grave robbing. Although it is unlikely, the remains could be from a homicide. Some animal bones can easily be mistaken as human bones. This determination becomes especially difficult when encountering fragmented bones. Agencies should contact a forensic anthropologist for determination of the origin of the bones.

Some practitioners will spew Chamba onto the Nganga using their mouth. Responders may discover burns inside the mouth due to the use of peppers in the liquid. Patients may also become ill if they ingest the Chamba.

References

1. Arostequi, Natalia Bolivar, Ta Makuende Yaya y las reglas de palo monte: Mayombe, brillumba, kimbisa, shamalongo, Cuba, Ediciones UNIÓN, Unión de Escritores y Artistas de Cuba, 1993.
2. McGaffey, Wyatt, *Astonishment and Power: The Eyes of Understanding Kongo Minkisi*, Washington, D.C., Smithsonian Institution, 1993.
3. Bockie, Simon, *Death and the Invisible Powers: The World of Kongo Belief*, Bloomington, Indiana University Press, 1993.
4. Thompson, Robert Ferris, *Flash of the Spirit: African and Afro-American Art and Philosophy*, New York, Vintage, 1984.

Voodoo

6

Assessing the Scene

> You receive a call to respond to a residence in which a 50-year-old Haitian female is having seizures. As you walk through the house to get to the patient, you notice a number of colorful statues and candles in the rooms. Walls are covered with images of Catholic saints while plants and various gourds hang from the ceilings. The patient is sitting on the floor that is inscribed with chalk circles and lines. A group of men and women dressed in white clothing stand against one of the walls where colored flags hang.

With the stigma that Hollywood has placed on the practice of Voodoo, the responder may have a sense of culture shock when encountering authentic Voodoo rituals. The word *Voodoo* itself invokes images of zombies, black magic and human sacrifice. The reality of Voodoo is something all together different. The real world of Voodoo is a complex religion that focuses on the spirits of ancestors as well as the spirits of nature that rule this world. Ancestor reverence of the practice can be traced back to Africa where many Africans still seek guidance and protection from their departed kin. The belief system of Voodoo serves as an old friend to those Haitian Americans who have come to live in America. Practiced still in the basements of Brooklyn and the kitchens of Miami, the Voodoo religion and its gods act as a comfort to Haitians who experience a totally new way of life in America.

Beliefs and Practices

The religion of Voodoo comes from Benin, formerly known as Dahomey, West Africa. The African beliefs and gods were challenged by the colonialists who took over the island of Hispaniola and imported slaves from this continent. The colonialists sought to destroy the African identity by forcing religious practices of Catholicism onto the Africans. To assimilate, the African people began to mix the European's view of religion with the practices of African traditional religion. The practices of several African groups, such as the Yoruba, Congo, Fon and Senegalese, evolved into Voodoo, which is a West African word that means "spirit."

The island of Hispaniola is composed of Haiti on the western third of the island and the Dominican Republic on the east. Voodoo was suppressed by colonialists in areas such as Haiti. However, today, Voodoo is *the* major religion of that country. While slavery in America sought to destroy Voodoo practices, it has managed to survive the onslaught of slavery and still exists in homes and temples across the United States.

Voodoo practitioners believe in a creator deity known as Gran Met Bondye. Gran Met means Great Master and Bondye comes from Bon Dieu, which means Good God.

The Voodoo belief system primarily focuses on the reverence of deities created by Bondye, known as Loas. The Loas are different manifestations of the creator deity and are often referred to as Mysteries or Angels. Adherents believe that the Loas come from a variety of African countries and ethnic groups. Because of this, the rituals and characteristics of these deities will differ. Loas are typically organized into groups according to their location of origin and their personality. These groups are called Nations. Some of the nations are the Petro, Rada, Congo and Nago. These spirits live in a city beneath the sea known as Ginen. They must be summoned into this world in order to manifest (appear or be revealed"). The Loas are also organized into "families." Some of the families, such as the Ogou, Ezili and Gede, have spirits that are known by the family name and the individual spirit name, such as Ezili Freda and Ezili Danto (Figure 6.1).[1]

Rada

The Loas that come from the holy city Arada of the Dahomey region of Africa are called Rada. Rada Loas are considered "cool" by followers. These spirits have friendly characteristics. The following spirits are part of the Rada pantheon:

Legba

Legba is the owner of the Crossroads and is called upon first in ceremonies to open the doorway to the spiritual world. Sometimes called Papa Legba, he is syncretized with Saint Peter, who guards the keys to heaven, and Saint Lazarus. His favorite color is red.

Marasa

These Loas are "sacred" twin spirits that appear in Rada and Petro rituals. The twins may be invoked following Legba in rituals. They may have other spirit offspring known as Marasa Dosu, which means "boy." The sacrifices are in the form of foods served in a terra cotta bowl called the Mange-Marasa. The bowl looks like three small bowls connected together. The Marasa are depicted as Saint Cosmo and Saint Damien.

Figure 6.1 This celebratory shrine contains many objects representing the deities of Haitian Voodoo. (Courtesy of Sallie Ann Glassman and Jeffrey Ehrenreich.)

Loko

Loko is known as the first priest (Houngan) and he guards the sanctuary (Peristyle). Loco is the Loa of healing with herbs. Loko is associated with the images of Saint Joseph and the archangel Gabriel. Offerings to Loco are placed in straw bags.

Ayizan

Ayizan is the wife of Legba and is depicted as an old woman with an apron that has deep pockets. She represents the marketplace and is sometimes referred to as the "mother of all initiates." Ayizan is represented by mounds of dirt surrounded by fringes of palm fronds.

Sobo

Sobo is the Loa of strength. He also rules over thunder and rain. Sobo acts as the judge of the temple and is depicted as a handsome soldier. He is symbolized by an emblem of lightning.

Agassou

The myth of Agassou tells of his birth from a princess and leopard. Agassou is referred to as the king of the Leopard Society of West Africa, a men's tribal society. He guards the traditions of Dahomey. Some Voodoo historians say that Agassou was the first human to develop into a Loa.

La Sirene

La Sirene is a fish-like being that lives and rules over the oceans. Married to the Loa Agwe, she is syncretized with La Diosa del Mar, and is represented by mirrors, combs, a small trumpet, pearls, perfume and items from the ocean.

Azaka

Azaka is referred to as the Country Cousin. He is a man from the country who represents agriculture, and is depicted as wearing the clothes of a farmer, such as denim pants and carrying a straw bag. Azaka is syncretized with Saint Isidore. His favorite colors are blue, red and green. He is represented by his straw sack and a tobacco pipe.

Damballah Wedo

Damballah Wedo is the Loa of goodness. In the Fon language, Damballah is called *Dan*, which refers to the royal serpent of Dahomey. Dan is the symbol of the origins of the kingdom of Dahomey and he is represented by a serpent. Damballah is syncretized with Saint Patrick. Symbolized by a snake and a rainbow, his favorite color is white, and his offerings include eggs, milk and champagne.

Ayida Wedo

Ayida Wedo is the Loa of wealth and happiness. She is represented by a serpent and a rainbow. Ayida Wedo is syncretized with Our Lady of Immaculate Conception. She is the wife of Damballah and her favorite colors are blue and white.

Ezili Freda

Also known as Ezili Maitresse, Ezili Freda is the Loa of love and luxury. She is represented by a heart and is syncretized with the Virgin Mary. Ezili is the wife of Legba and her favorite colors are blue and pink. She is symbolized by a heart and a mirror and is given offerings of sweet desserts, perfumes and flowers.

Ogou Group

The Ogous are powerful warriors. Ogou (which stands for justice) is the Loa of blacksmiths and is symbolized by a sword stuck in the ground. An Ogou is also represented by an iron rod stuck in the fire. There are several manifestations of Ogous, and they are syncretized with Saint James the Greater. An Ogou's favorite color is red.

Agwe

Agwe is the Loa of the ocean. He is the patron of sailors and fishermen and is represented by a boat. Agwe is syncretized with Saint Ulrich. His offerings are placed on small boats and his favorite colors are white, green and pink.

Petro

The Loas that come from the colony of Saint Domingue are known as Petro Loa. The Petros take their name from a man called Don Pedro who lived in the 1700s. Don Pedro promoted several distinct dances and ceremonies. The Petro Loas are known as "fiery" and sometimes malevolent spirits. The Petro spirits may be used in sorcery and can be summoned with gunpowder and the cracking of bullwhips.

Some of the Petro spirits are discussed below.

Simbi

Simbi are a group of ancestral spirits. These spirits live in the water that separates the land of the living and the land of the dead. The Loa of Clairvoyance, Simbi is represented by a pond of water and is syncretized with the Magi that visited Christ. Simbi's favorite colors are black and grey and they are represented by a pond and slim snakes.

Kalfu (Carrefour)

Kalfu is the Petro Loa of Legba. Kalfu allows bad luck and evil to enter the world through the crossroads. His symbol is the moon and he may be used in malevolent magic.

Gran Bwa

Gran Bwa is creole for Great Tree. Gran Bwa is the protector of wildlife. He is the lord over the forest and jungle and assists in healing and initiation. He is represented by a tree with a cloth wrapped around it. Gran Bwa presides over the ritual of the grinding of herbs known as Pile Fey.

Ezili Danto (Erzulie Dantor)

Also known as Ezili of the Red Eyes, Ezili Danto is the wife of Ti-Jean Petro and Simbi Makaya. She is syncretized with Mater Salvatoris or Our Lady of Chestochowa, sometimes known as the African Saint Barbara. She protects single mothers and children. Her images depict her holding her child named Anais. Scars on her face are from her rivalry with Ezili Freda. She is symbolized by a dagger and bowls of blood.

Marinette-Bwa-Chech

Marinette is the principal female Loa of the Petro pantheon. She is a wife to Ti-Jean Petro and is represented by a screeching owl. She is a vicious spirit that is syncretized with Anima Sola and can free someone from or take them into bondage. Her colors are black and blood red. Marinette is believed to be the Mambo who sacrificed the black pig that started the first Haitian revolution.

Ti-Jean Petro

Ti-Jean Petro is a spirit that roams through the bush. He is depicted as a dwarf with one foot. This spirit protects sorcerers. He is the son of Erzulie Dantor (Ezili Danto) as well as her lover.

Simbi

These are the Simbi that are also followed in the Rada pantheon of Loa. These Simbi are a family of serpent Loa from the Kongo region. They include Loa, such as Simbi Andezo, Simbi Makaya, Simbi Dlo an Gran Simbi. They are utilized in Voodoo secret societies much like in the Sanpwel secret society.

Gede

The Gede family is a group of Loa that rule over the cemeteries. The Gede are symbolized by a cross that represents the "crossroads." These Loa have distinguishing characteristics in ritual, dance and sacrifices. The Gede family of spirits include spirits, such as Gede Nibo, Gede Plumaj, Gede Ti Mails and Gede Zaranye. The Gede are led by the Baron spirits of the dead. Initiates that become possessed by the Gede are characterized by a nasal tone of voice and the appearance of a dead man. The Gede use colors of black, purple and white.

Baron Samedi

Baron Samedi is the master over the cemeteries and is depicted dressed in black clothes with a black hat and dark glasses. He has a skull for a face and is represented on altars by phallic symbols. The Haitian dictator Papa Doc (François) Duvalier dressed as Baron Samedi in most of his public appearances. Baron Samedi's other manifestations include Baron La Croix, Baron Cimitere and Baron Criminel. His colors are black and purple.

Maman Brigette

Maman Brigette is the wife of Baron Samedi. Brigette is the mother of all spirits who enter this world. The graveyard is considered her "womb." She is the female guardian of graves and is syncretized with Saint Bridget.

Spiritual Bodies and Guardians

Voodoo belief teaches that human beings have two distinct spiritual bodies. The first is known as the Ti-Bon-Anj (Ti-Bon-Ange), which means the "little good angel." This is the consciousness. The Ti-Bon-Anj leaves the body during sleep or in trance possession. The second spiritual body is known as the Gros-Bon-Anj, which means the "Big good angel." This body is the "psyche" of the individual and is part of the divine in man. The Gros-Bon-Anj keeps humans alive.

Voodoo teaches that everyone has a Loa that guards him or her. The Met Tet means "the master of the head." This is similar to a guardian angel. The Loa may reveal themselves through dreams or through possessing the individual. The priest or priestess may identify the Loa during the Kanzo ritual.

Group Structure

The hierarchy of practitioners in Voodoo ranges from the brief associate to the full-time priest or priestess. There are those practitioners who have not been initiated, but attend ceremonies and go to the priesthood for wisdom. These practitioners are known as Vodouisant. An uninitiated practitioner who attends ceremonies and is preparing for initiation is known as the Hounsi, which means "bride of the spirit."

The first stage of initiation is known as the Hounsi Kanzo. Initiates become "married" to a spirit. The second stage is known as As Si Pwen or Sur Point. This means the initiate is serving one particular Loa. The initiate is permitted to use the Asson, which is the sacred rattle used to invoke the Loa. The initiate may lead prayers and songs in the temple and, at this level, may initiate others into this level of initiation. Also, initiates at this stage are taught how to care for the Loa.

The third and final stage of initiation is called Asogwe. Initiates at this point have become priests and priestesses of the Voodoo faith and can confirm initiations of all stages on other initiates. The priestess in Voodoo is known as the Mambo and the priest is known as the Houngan (Figure 6.2). Initiates may refer to this clergy as Mama or Papa. The priest and priestess may oversee a group of believers known as a Society. This is a group that meets at various times for worship and ritual.

There are also a number of "specialized" offices in the Voodoo society, including choir director, animal keeper and others. Some types of priests

Figure 6.2 The priest (Houngan) and the priestess (Mambo) perform sacred baths using herbs and water. (Photo courtesy of Sallie Ann Glassman and Jeffrey Ehrenreich.)

have a special title according to their specialty. The Bokor is a priest who works with the spirits of the dead. Some practitioners use the term "left hand" to describe the malevolent work that a Bokor can perform.

There are also a number of secret societies that exist in Haitian Voodoo. These societies may worship a particular deity or follow a particular religious tradition.

Ritual Tools[2]

Asson

The Asson is a rattle similar to a maraca and is usually carried by those who have been initiated into a priest or priestess position of leadership. This rattle is usually made from a large calabash. It is sometimes filled and covered with

Figure 6.3 The priestess, known as the Mambo, takes the rattle called an Asson. Use of the Asson is restricted to initiated clergy in the religion. (Photo courtesy of Sallie Ann Glassman and Jeffrey Ehrenreich.)

snake vertebrae or glass beads. The rattler may be used to strike the Veve signatures of the spirits (Figure 6.3).

Bottle

Bottles covered in sequins, beads and fabric are used in many rituals. The bottles are decorated in colors representing the Loa and also may be decorated with an image of a saint. Bottles are used to honor the Loa. Some may hold offerings while some bottles that are decorated with doll heads may be used in divination rites.

Chromolithograph

Chromolithographs are images of the Loa represented in Catholic saint form.

Flags

Multicolored flags known as Drapo may be found during a search or observation of a residence in which Voodoo is practiced. Flags announce the spirits that will attend a ceremony. Voudon flags are usually made of fine cloth with sequined images of the spirits sewn into them. Flags may be kept on the Pe (or central pole of the temple) to give them power.

Govi

A spirit can be called through a vessel of water using a white sheet of cloth. It is then placed inside a jar called a Govi, which is used to call down the Loa. These jars are found in the temple and may be decorated with symbols of the Loa.

Packets

The Packet comes from the Congo region. The Packet is a bag that contains bones, herbs, stones and other ingredients. The bag, usually decorated with satin cloth and sequins, may have one stem sticking out of it. This is a male packet. Female packets will have two arms rounded pointing down. The packet is found in the temple and is used to "heat up" the Loa for ceremonies. The packet is also known as a Wanga.

Swords

Swords are used in Voudoo rituals as symbols of the iron spirit Ogou. There is a ritual procession of the sword known as the Sword of La Place. The La Place is the sword bearer who helps begin the rituals of Voodoo.

Ogan

The Ogan is a cowbell-type instrument without a clapper. It is struck during ceremonies to summon the spirits.

The Triangle

An iron triangle that is a musical instrument is used in rituals as well. When it is struck, it opens spiritual doorways.

Conch Shell

The conch shell is blown like a trumpet to call the Loa of the ocean, Agwe.

Zins

Zins are three-legged pots. They are filled with oil and set on fire. The fire from the pots is used to warm the Loas and increase their power (Figure 6.4).

Drums

Drums are a core piece of equipment in a Voudon ceremony. The rhythms that are played on them call the spirits into the ceremony. The creation and preparation of the drums is a very developed ceremony and they are considered "alive." The drums are broken into different categories, according to the type of spirit being called. The three types of drums are Rada, Petro and Congo. Each drum has its own particular style of play and each has its own physical characteristics.

The three drums are described in detail below.

Rada drums are three in a set. Rada drums will typically have small pegs that stick out the sides of the top of the drum.

Petro drums come in sets of two with one drum larger than the other. The Petro do not contain pegs.

Congo drums usually come in sets of three.

Figure 6.4 The three-legged pot known as the Zin is filled with oil and burnt as a lamp. The pot is used to "warm" the Loa. (Courtesy of Michael Vincent, Orange County Sheriff's Office Criminal Investigations, Orlando, Florida.)

Drums are treated as living beings and are given power and even fed sacrificed animals.

Ceremonies

Voodoo ceremonies are referred to as "services." The service is performed to contact the Loa. Practices and artifacts are used to "heat things up" (Echofe) to summon the Loa. Offerings of food, animals and songs are presented in hopes that the Loa will come to the ceremony. The traditional Voodoo ceremony has several components that must occur before the Loa appear to the temple. The two main parts of the service are the procession of the

Figure 6.5 A mural of a traditional Voodoo ceremony.

flags, drums and sacred ritual tools to the temple, and the invocations of Loa (Figure 6.5).

Entrance

The ceremony begins with the parade of the Houmphors flags. These flags are decorated with the symbols of the Loa. The Houmphors drums are then greeted. The center of the temple is entered and the four points of North, South, East and West are recognized. The Loa are called upon as well as the Catholic saints. Drumming and dancing begins to call the Loa. The Veve (religious symbols for the Loa) are drawn in cornmeal and powders on the ground to represent the Loa that are manifesting. The rituals begin with a prayer to Legba to open the gates to the spiritual world.

The Priye Ginen

The Priye Ginen or Prayer of Africa is used to open Voodoo services. The prayer is sung in French, Creole and African languages. The prayer creates sacred space for the ritual.

Manje Loa: The Sacrifice

The Loa are believed to eat as human beings do. The second part of the service is known as Manje Loa, this is the ritual feeding of the animals. Plates of food and animals to be sacrificed are left at the Poteau Mitan. The animals are dressed in colors of the Loa. The person in charge of the sacrifice (Commanditaire) usually wears a red cloth on his or her head. He/she eats some of the food on the plates and feeds the animals some of the food. If the animals eat the food, this means that animal has accepted the sacrifice. The animal is then rubbed with sacred herbs and killed. The person who kills it drinks some of the animal's blood and then carries it to the four points of the ritual area. Devotees may rub the animal's blood on their foreheads in the shape of crosses. The animals are then taken outside to be cooked.

The Loas have specific foods that they prefer. Some of the food offered to the Loas include:

Legba: cassavas, rice, green bananas, smoked foods, molted roosters
Azaka: corn, breads, unrefined sugar, brandy
Gede Family: black goats and black roosters
Baron Samdi: black goats, black hens
Dambala: eggs, rice, white hens
Ayida Wedo: white hens, rice, milk
Ezili: rice, chickens
Ezili Danto: fried pork
Ogou Feray: red roosters, bulls
Agwe: white sheep, hens, champagne
Simbi: black animals, turkeys, hens

Rites of Passage

There is a ceremony known as the Leve nom in which the initiate receives the name of an ancestor for protection. The ritual of Garde may be performed after the Leve nom. The Garde is a ritual of the cutting into the skin of the practitioner. The cut is a symbol that is used to identify members of the temple. Dried herbs may be rubbed into the cut to give protection to the initiate and then he/she gives offerings in exchange for the protection of the deity.

A ritual called Lave tet is a ritualistic washing of the head, which makes trance possession easier on the initiate. Later an initiate may receive a "refreshing" of the head called Rafraichi tete to widen the path for the spirit to work inside the initiate.

To become an initiated priest or priestess, a ceremony is performed called Haussement or the "lifting" of the initiate. The ritual is a lifting of the devotee in a chair three times and an oath is presented in which the initiate swears allegiance to the Loa.

Spirit Possession

Possession is a normative practice that temples observe. The initiate is "mounted" as in Santeria by the Loa. The initiate actually becomes possessed by the Loa and takes on the characteristics of the Loa. For example, those possessed by the Loa Dambala may act like a snake. Possession by Ogou will usually make the initiate wield a sword. Devotees who are possessed or "ridden" by the Gede Loa will wear sunglasses, a hat and will be given strong drinks like rum. The possession by the Gede spirits is usually marked by the initiate cursing and acting sexually promiscuous. The Loa will often speak through the possessed.

Initiation

The initiated is called the Ounsi. The ritual to becoming Ounsi takes one to two weeks. The initiate is dressed in white and is taught about the Loa and how to function in the temple. He or she is then presented to the temple. If the initiate becomes possessed, it is a sign that the initiate is connected to the Loa.

Marriage

Initiates can be married to the Loa in a ceremony. This is to give the initiate additional power from the Loa. The initiate is married in a traditional-type marriage ceremony where the initiate signs a marriage certificate to the Loa.

Zombies

The concept of Zombies in Haitian Voodoo is found in two forms. The first is through a magical being known as an "astral zombie," which is a captured soul that has no body.

The second concept of the zombie is probably the closest to the Hollywood image of the living dead. The zombie is a person who is being punished by a Houngan (first priest) or a Bokor (priest who works with the dead). The priest uses a process that involves using chemicals and derivatives from animals, such as the puffer fish and tree frogs. The chemicals are incorporated with a series of rituals that give the substances "magical essence." The powders used to create the zombie-like state have been compared to a form of anesthesia in which the victim's heart rate may drop drastically. The threat of becoming a zombie may be used as a punishment in some Voudon houses. Responders who are dealing with patients with this fear need to recognize this concern in the patient.

Sacred Days

The sacred days used by the Catholic Church are honored by the liturgical calendar of Voodoo practitioners.

Bains De Chance: "luck baths" on Christmas; from December 24 to January 6, herbs are crushed and the creation of sacred baths using them takes place during the Pile Fey.
January 6: Epiphany
July 16: Our Lady of Mt. Carmel is celebrated in honor of Ezili
July 25: St. James, Ogou
July 26: St. Anne, mother of Ezili
November 2: Fet Ghede, all souls day; go to cemetery, give offerings

Sacred Spaces

Voodoo temples throughout the United States appear to exist in two forms. The first being a traditional temple that is not only open to the public, but is also very public in the eye of the media and the local community. The second type of temple is usually hidden from the public view and may exist in the basements and storage buildings of Voodoo practitioners. If responders encounter a temple, there are a few common structural aspects the responders should be aware of that are used in the temple.

The Voodoo temple is called the Houmfort. The main ritual area in which the majority of ceremonies occur is called the Peristyle, which is usually decorated with drawings of the saints, hanging calabashes (hard-shelled gourds) and items representing the Loas. There is usually an area that contains a fire pit wherein resides an iron bar that represents the spirit of iron. In the center of the Peristyle is a pole called the Poteau Mitan. This is a French word meaning "pole in the middle." It used by the Loa to climb down from the heavens and the pole represents the center of the universe. It is usually decorated with paintings of the serpents Danbhalah and Aida Wedo.

One of the most common items found in the Voodoo ceremony is the Veve. This image originally came from the Congo region. The Congo religions utilize drawings and symbols in much of their ceremonies and rites. This is an image that is universally recognized as the symbol of a particular Loa. The symbol is drawn on the ground with cornmeal, coffee, powdered brick or chalk. His figure is usually placed where a spirit is to manifest with food, sometimes being left on the drawings for the spirit. The Veve is a doorway for the Loa to appear through.

There is also an altar called the Pe. The Pe is usually square shaped and holds several personal ritual objects that are considered sacred to the members of the temple. This may even include a snake representing Danbhala, the serpent god.

The temple also contains chambers known as Kay Miste or Huts of the Mysteries, which are reserved for worship of a single Loa. These chambers may contain images and tools used by the particular Loa.

Responders may also encounter altars and shrines containing a number of items in the homes of practitioners. The personal altar is called a Rogatoire, which usually contains a picture of the saint that corresponds with their personal Loa. Candles, crosses and other Voudon icons may be on this altar. Food may be left on the altar for the Loa as well.

Many of the items frequently found on a traditional Voodoo altar include:

Lithographs or prints of Catholic saints
Ceramic or terra cotta pots
Drinking glass or shot glass of rum or wine
Bottles of rum, champagne
Statues

Objects representing the Loa also are found on the altar. Each Loa has several artifacts that reflect the personality of each individual Loa.

Azaka is represented by a straw bag and tobacco pipe. The bag, known as the Alfo, is worn much like a purse. The items of Azaka reflect his personality as a Haitian farmer.
Agwe is represented by a wooden boat that hangs from the ceiling.
The **Ogou Loa** may be represented by a sword and objects of iron.
La Siren may be represented by images of mermaids and seashells. She may also be represented by combs and mirrors.
Legba may be represented by a wooden crutch and tobacco pipes.
Ezili Danto is represented by a knife, which is frequently placed inside a bowl.
The **Baron Loa** may be represented by a black top hat.
The **Gede** family of spirits is represented by a coffin, sunglasses and a cross. Images of skulls may also be used for Gede.
Ezili Freda may be represented by jewelry, perfume and lace.

Western culture also contributes to the altars and shrines of the Voodoo practitioner. Toy action figures and photographs of American pop icons may be placed there. To outsiders the altars may appear strange and unorganized, but to the creator and owner of the altar, the elements all have significance. The strength of the god Legba may be symbolized with a Batman action figure while the female gender of the spirit Ezili may be represented by a Barbie doll. Significance is in the eye of the beholder.

Health and Sickness

The Loa can inflict punishment on those who they are disciplining. If an initiate is neglecting the Loa or is being careless, the Loa can punish through violent trance possession.

A phenomenon, known as a Baka, can affect a client. The Baka is an evil spirit that is sent to do harm to someone.

Since we are looking specifically at Haitian Voodoo, it is important as well to look at the Haitian culture, which teaches that sickness can come from one of two sources. Maladi Pei is a term to describe "country illnesses" that come on naturally. Maladi Bon Die refers to an illness of a spiritual nature. These "diseases of the Lord" must be approached holistically through physical and spiritual means. The concept of "hot" and "cold" blood is a condition believed to affect the patient's health.

There are several Haitian folk sicknesses or culture-bound sicknesses. Some of the Haitian culture-bound sicknesses include:

Pedisyon (perdition): Woman thought to be pregnant, but blood flows to menstrual blood and pregnancy is paused.

Mal Dyok (Maldjok) is the evil eye; caused by envy.

Seziman is fright caused by stress.

Giyon is bad luck caused by someone directing bad vibrations toward an initiate.

Some illnesses specific to the Voodoo culture include:

A sickness may be a result of the Loa feeling neglected. The initiate may have disregarded giving offerings to his/her personal Loa. Illness is a way to get the attention of the initiate.

Anvwa Mo means "sending the dead." An enemy may send the dead to attack a client. The spirit of the dead, known as the Mo, attaches itself to the victim. The Baron of the Ghede is called to tell the priest about the dead. The client is placed on a mat made from leaves and the Baron is given offerings of rum, candles and wood.

The Ti-Bon-Ange (Ti-Bon-Anj; little good angel) can be captured by sorcery.[3]

Healing techniques can include baths, massages and potions or the patient may be encouraged to spend time in the temple. One ritual technique involves placing the protection of a particular Loa over an individual. The Garde is a ceremonial act in which a cut is made into the arm of the patient and then rubbed with various herbs.

At the time of death, the Ti-Bon-Ange is believed to travel to the world of the Invisibles. After a year and a day the spirit returns to humanity. The spirit is brought back in a ceremony known as Return of the Dead from the Water, and is then placed in the Govi jar.

Some patients may have trouble obtaining help from local Voudon clergy (Houngan and Mambo) because of lack of funds. Some Voudon clergy charge large fees to perform healing rituals. However, once clergy is secured for healing work, the healer may use divination to determine the source of sickness.

There are several other offices of folk healers in the Haitian and Haitian Voodoo communities, including herbalists known as Docte Fey, midwives known as Matrons and bone setters known as Docte Zo.

Other Traditions of Voodoo

Responders may encounter practitioners of other traditions of Voodoo. A patient that simply uses the term *Voodoo* when describing their personal religious practices does not necessarily mean that they are describing traditional Haitian Voodoo.

Dominican Voodoo (21 Divisiones)

The Dominican Republic shares the island of Hispaniola with Haiti. Voodoo from the Dominican Republic has a different "flavor" to its beliefs and practices. With many similar aspects, such as the use of the term *Loa*, Dominican Voodoo practitioners refer to a creator named Papa Bon Dye and the Loa as the 21 Divisiones. Dominican Voodoo includes some Loa that are distinctive from the Dominican geographical region, such as Anaisa Pye and Candelo Cedife.

Dahomean or West African Voodoo

West African Voodoo relies on the deities and practices of Voodoo *before* the religion traveled to areas such as Haiti. The rituals and practices are said by practitioners to be the oldest examples of the Voudon religion in the world. The Loas are referred to as Spirits. Some levels of initiation in West African Voodoo can be attained only through birthright and inheritance.

New Orleans Voodoo

New Orleans Voodoo is an interesting phenomenon. Its tradition is perhaps the most accessible to the general public. Based on personal research and academic texts, the tradition of New Orleans Voodoo appears to have

Figure 6.6 An altar dedicated to those lost in the tragedy of Hurricane Katrina. (Photo courtesy of Sallie Ann Glassman and Jeffrey Ehrenreich.)

two "faces." There is an unstructured collective group of practices that contains commercialized icons, such as voodoo dolls, zombie images and snake worship items. This tradition does not appear to be typically embraced as a serious practice by practitioners. However, there is a second tradition of New Orleans Voodoo that is a sophisticated system that uses the practices of Haitian Voodoo, Southern folk magic and Spiritism. As one practitioner explains, "It's like a spiritual gumbo. You use a little bit of everything in your practices" (Figure 6.6).[4]

Responder Issues

The growth of traditional Voodoo is becoming popular among nongenerational practitioners. However, Voodoo in its purest form is found primarily among those who have come from Haiti and the areas of Africa where it is a common family religion. Officers that have a background in dealing with the Haitian population will most likely see the subtle outward signs of traditional Voodoo. Officers should be reminded that Voodoo is a very rich tradition among Haitian families and is considered sacred. Intelligence on criminal activities from this community might be difficult to obtain.

Florida Water is a substance used in Voodoo rites for cleansing rituals. It is a widely available "perfume" that is made from various floral oils and alcohol. A 1998 *New York Times* article reported that a Haitian immigrant from Long Island, New York, sought out the services of a Voodoo priest to perform a ritual cleansing on her. The priest covered the lady with a sheet and began to douse her with Florida Water cologne to rid her of evil spirits. The priest then set the sheet on fire, which immediately lit the flammable cologne and left the lady with third degree burns on her face.[5] Responders should be aware of the uses of Florida Water and other ritual liquids that can be flammable if exposed to heat.

Responders may discover cuts on the patient. The ritual Garde may be evident on the patient's skin. One Mambo communicated to me that the cut may appear like raised scar tissue.

Several objects are considered sacred and officers are advised to use caution when handling them. Handling these objects in front of practitioners could produce violent behavior. If an officer must investigate items, it is suggested that he/she keep practitioners away from the area.

Some aspects of trance possession can include possible harmful activities. It is said that initiates who become possessed by the Loa Ezili Je Wouj, also known as Red Eyes, will rub red pepper in their eyes during possession.

Officers encountering rituals may find several tools, such as swords and blades, that are used in the ceremony. Always use caution when entering ceremony areas.

Law enforcement personnel may arrive during a spirit possession. If possible allow the leader of the group to stop the possession. Remove followers from the ritual area when touching the possessed subject.

Officers should use caution when examining altars and ritual jars and bottles. Toxic powders may be present and can cause damage to the investigating officer.

Officers should also be aware of state animal statutes regarding use of animals in religious sacrifices.

Again, respect tempered with caution is the rule. Be sure that you have sufficient probable cause or a real emergency before disturbing *any* religious ceremony.

References

1. Brown, Karen McCarthey, *Mama Lola: A Voudou Priestess in Brooklyn,* Berkeley, University of California Press, 2001.
2. Consentino, Donald J., *Sacred Arts of Haitian Voudou,* Los Angeles, California, University of Los Angeles Fowler Museum, 1995.
3. Personal communication with Houngan Hector, leader of Sosyete Gade Nou Leve, Sicklerville, New Jersey.
4. Personal communication with Mambo Sallie Glassman, La Source Ancienne Ounfo, New Orleans, Louisiana.
5. *New York Times,* 1998. A Voodoo priest is charged with burning of a woman. April 8.

Curanderismo

7

Assessing the Scene

> You and your partner are transporting an elderly female patient to the emergency room. The patient begins to complain of chest pains and starts to cry, "Empacho, Empacho." As you check the patient's vitals, you notice that she is clutching a small red and black bracelet.

Responders who encounter practitioners of Curanderismo will find a diverse collection of folk treatments that have survived throughout history in the Latin community.

Curanderismo is a blanket term used to describe the traditional folk healing practices of Mexican and Spanish American communities. The name Curanderismo comes from a Spanish word *Currar,* which means "to heal." Curanderismo mixes cultural aspects of Aztec, African, Native American and European witchcraft religious cultures.

Curanderismo may be utilized by members of various faiths, but it does not hold its participants to a particular dogma or sacred text. Curanderismo is an alternative method of healing for many in the Hispanic community. It is more accurate to describe Curanderismo as a practice that works alongside religion other than being a religion unto itself.

Beliefs and Practices

Practitioners of Curanderismo typically are Catholic and recognize the deity of the Christian God as well as the saints of the Catholic Church. The saints are recognized as spiritual helpers along with a number of "folk saints" (Figure 7.1). These saints are spiritual "personalities" that originate with the combination of Spanish Catholic saints and regional indigenous beliefs.[1]

Folk saints, such as Our Lady of Guadalupe, are recognized for their historical and spiritual legacies (Figure 7.2). Each folk saint has the ability to grant spiritual powers to those that call upon him/her. For example, Saint Martin de Porres is a folk saint recognized for helping the poor. His mythology tells of his mercy toward a poor man and how he was rewarded by God for

Figure 7.1 An altar dedicated to the folk saints of Curanderismo.

his service. Today followers of Curanderismo may place his picture in their homes as an object of hope that they may receive riches and avoid poverty.

There are a number of folk saints that are recognized in the practice of Curanderismo (Figure 7.3). Following are some of the saints and their characteristics.

Our Lady of Guadalupe

One of the most popular folk saints of Curanderismo is Our Lady of Guadalupe. She appeared as a manifestation of the Virgin Mary to a peasant named Juan Diego on the hill of Tonantzin near Mexico City. The legend surrounding the Virgin is that she told Juan Diego to build a temple to her and to tell others about her appearance, Miraculously, roses began to grow and Juan was told to pick them. An image of Mary also appeared on the cloak of Juan Diego. The Virgin is honored every year with a pilgrimage to the spot where she appeared. Some believe that she is the modern manifestation of an Aztec goddess. Curanderismo teaches that she will answer prayers and wipe the tears from her followers' eyes.

Figure 7.2 An altar dedicated to Our Lady of Guadalupe. Some believe the saint to be the reincarnation of an Aztec goddess known as Tonantzin. The spiritual work performed using this figure combines aspects of the Catholic faith and magical rites found in European witchcraft and African traditional religions.

San Martin de Porres

San Martin was a Dominican friar who gave selflessly to help others. He established an orphanage for children and a hospital for children. Followers pray to him for help with finances.

San Martin Caballero

San Martin Caballero was a centurion in the Roman army. One day, San Martin was riding his horse and came upon a beggar. The beggar had no clothes, so San Martin tore his cloak and gave half of it to the beggar. That evening San Martin had a dream that the beggar turned into Jesus. San Martin left the army and became a monk. San Martin will help followers by bringing strangers to give aid to his followers. Some businesses will display images of San Martin Caballero (Figure 7.4).

Figure 7.3 Responders may encounter statues of folk saints and offerings to the spirits that they represent.

Figure 7.4 Folk saints, such as San Martin Caballero, bring good fortune to those who honor him in their homes and businesses.

Judas Tudeo

Also known as Saint Jude, Judas Tudeo is a relative of Jesus. His name means "Praises given to God" and "Brave to proclaim the faith." Followers pray to him because he is the saint of impossible causes. One informant claims that people pray to Saint Jude for jobs and opportunities to work.

Santa Marta

Santa Marta is a saint who was known for taming a crocodile and, in some legends, a dragon. Marta is called upon to break women of infidelity and to command or compel a person to do your bidding. Some sources list her as a source of fierce protection.

San Simon

Also known as Maximon, San Simon is depicted as a man in a dark suit and hat. He is usually depicted as sitting in a chair. Cultural researchers note that San Simon is actually a Pre-Columbian Mayan deity. He is given offerings of Coca-Cola, cigarettes and alcohol. He provides financial success to those who pray to him.

Jesus Malverde

Jesus Malverde was a Mexican bandit who was hanged by police in 1909. The image of Malverde is honored as the "narco-saint" by members of the drug trade. His image depicts the mustached bandit sitting in a chair or standing.

Juan Soldado

Juan Soldado is a folk saint who is honored primarily in Mexico and in the Southwestern United States. Soldado was a Mexican soldier who was falsely accused of the rape and murder of a young girl. Soldado was executed for the girl's death. His image is revered for providing good health and protection for immigrants crossing the United States–Mexico border.

Dr. Jose Gregorio Hernandez

Dr. Jose Gregorio Hernandez is a folk saint who is honored for his healing powers. Hernandez, commonly known as Jose Gregorio, was a Venezuelan physician who provided healthcare to impoverished patients free of charge. After his death, Hernandez became elevated to the status of a saint by local communities.

San Toribio Romo

Toribio Romo is a folk saint who is honored on altars and in shrines for his power to protect immigrants from authorities. Romo was a Catholic priest who was killed in 1928 by Mexican soldiers. His reputation as a benevolent giver to the poor and hungry is still honored by his followers.

Figure 7.5 Santa Muerte is a folk saint who is reported to be honored as the patron saint of criminals. Her icon has been found in several cases involving narcotics traffickers who insist that she provides them protection from the law.

Santa Muerte

Santa Muerte is also known as Santisima Muerte and The Lady in White. Controversy surrounds the exact origin of this folk saint. Some historians have connected her image to an Aztec deity while some believe she is an inversion of the Lady of Guadalupe. She is depicted as a skeleton with the clothing of the Virgin Mary. Offerings of apples, coins, flowers and perfumes are given to her. She is also the subject of controversy because she is used by narco traffickers (drug dealers) in Mexico. Many use her image because they believe she is simply a folk saint who relates to the poor and downtrodden (Figure 7.5).

Other Folk Saints

Practitioners of Curanderismo also recognize a special group of folk healers who were elevated to sainthood by locals who knew them. The three healers, known as Los Tres Grandes or Three Great Ones, are Don Pedrito Jaramillo, Nino Fidencio and Teresita Urrea. These three figures were recognized as being gifted healers who served mankind with special spiritual gifts and can still be accessed by practitioners.

Don Pedrito Jaramillo was known as the Saint of Falfarrias. He was born in 1829 in Mexico. He learned that he had the gift of healing when he fell from a horse and was able to heal himself. People from all over the country traveled to be healed by Don Pedrito until he died in 1907. His shrine in Falfarrias, Texas, is visited every year by thousands of followers who pay homage to this folk saint.

Nino Fidencio was born in Mexico in 1898. He worked with a German doctor for years during which time he discovered his ability to heal. Followers, known as Fidencistas, travel to his shrine every year to be healed. Some spiritualists believe that they can "channel" the spirit of Nino to heal others.

Teresita Urrea was known as the Saint of Cabora. Born in Mexico in 1873, Teresita was an apprentice to a Curandera (female healer). She was attacked by a man and almost raped. She lapsed into a coma and those around her thought she was dead and prepared for her funeral. She suddenly awoke from the coma and three days later her mentor died. Teresita took her place and became famous as a healer. She was involved in encouraging the Yaqui Indians to fight for their homeland. Many followers, known as Teresistas, wore images of her on their clothing during battles with the government. Teresista died in exile in the United States in 1906 at the age of 33, allegedly from overwork.

Group Structure

The central figure that provides healing in Curanderismo is the Curandero (females are known as Curanderas). These healers use special spiritual abilities to heal others. These abilities are called El Don de Dios or Gift from God.[2] The gift to heal may be something that the Curandero or Curandera is born with. Some children are recognized as being potential healers from a very young age. Some Curanderos do not realize their gift of healing until they receive a spiritual "calling" in their lives. Some healers are simply individuals who become apprentices to established healers in the community.

The role of the Curandero plays a very important part in the life of the community. He acts as a counselor, doctor and even exorcist. The Curandero may be very public about his role as a healer or he may be known only to certain members in the community. Publicly known Curanderos may operate spiritual supply stores known as Botanicas or Yerberas (Figure 7.6). Some Curanderos are very discreet about their presence in the local community. Misunderstanding by outside cultures and the unregulated prescription of treatments are just a few of the reasons that some remain secretive about their presence. One Curandero who was interviewed explained that his reason for not advertising his services was that he relied on word of mouth from members of the Hispanic community and that the established healthcare industry would try to shut him down. The Curandero said, "The hospital charges thousands of dollars for what I can do for little or no money."

Curanderos may also call on the assistance of additional "specialists" in folk healing. The Sobadora is a therapeutic masseuse who can apply mas-

Figure 7.6 Amulets and talismans are sold by the Curandero/Curandera to provide health and healing.

Figure 7.7 Herbs may be prescribed by a Yerbero who serves as an herbal specialist to the Hispanic community.

sage techniques to aching muscles. The Yerbero provides specialized herbal treatments for patients (Figure 7.7). The Albolaius specializes in combating witchcraft or Brujeria in patients who have been cursed. The Partera serves as a midwife who provides services for women in labor. The office of Huesero sets bones for those who have injuries to bone structure.

Healing and Sickness

There are a number of illnesses that are brought about by natural phenomena as well as a number that come by supernatural means. The Curandero may prescribe treatments to sicknesses that are classified as "folk illnesses."

One of the main principles that the Curanderismo observes comes from the Greek concept of wellness. The Greek concept of "humors" teaches that the human body has a certain balance of "hot" and "cold" principles.[3] These principles can be thrown off by various illnesses. Low metabolic rates resulting from colds and pneumonia may affect the cold concept. High metabolic rates from shock and diabetes may affect the hot concept. The treatment philosophy is to approach the cold's imbalance with a hot remedy. Likewise, the hot imbalance is treated with a cold treatment.

The goal is to restore harmony to these concepts. This may be resolved using teas, oils, herbs and foods.

There are a number of common folk illnesses recognized by their folk names. The following are some of the more widely recognized illnesses:

Mal Aire: This sickness is caused by exposure to air. Symptoms include nausea, vomiting, headaches, twitching of facial muscles and chills.

Empacho: This sickness is caused by food being trapped in the intestinal wall. Symptoms include constipation, loss of appetite and bloating.

Caida de Mollera: Also known as Fallen Fontanelle. This sickness is caused by the fontanelle (soft spot on newborn's head) caving in on the soft palate. Some believe this condition is caused by a mother removing her child from her breast during breastfeeding. Symptoms include colic and loss of appetite.

Encono: Also known as Festering of Wounds. This is caused by infections to a wound by interacting with someone. Symptoms include worsening of a wound.

Mal de Ojo: Also known as the Evil Eye. The evil eye is a concept that is observed by many different world cultures. The concept is that someone can inflict harm by looking upon someone with envy. This envy may manifest either intentionally or unintentionally. A casual admiration at a child can cause Mal de Ojo. Symptoms include physical or emotional sickness.

Malificia: Also known as Witchcraft or Brujeria. Sickness caused by malevolent magic or curses against someone. Symptoms include emotional and physical disturbances and disease.

Melarchico: Also known as Melancholy. Sickness caused by change in the environment. Symptoms include loss of appetite and depression.

Susto: Also known as Fright or Shock. Sickness caused by an emotional shock. Symptoms include depression, insomnia and nightmares.

Billis: Sickness caused by suppressed anger. Symptoms include excessive bile, headache, tension and gastrointestinal sickness.
Mal de Latido: Palpitations symptoms in the chest; pulsating of the stomach.
Sangre Debil: Also known as Tired Blood. Symptoms include poor appetite, weakness, and increased sleep.
Insolacion: Symptoms are similar to sunstroke.

Most of the folk illnesses can be interpreted with traditional Western medical labels by responders. For example, the *empacho* may be indigestion or possible chest pains. The *mal aire* could be sinus problems or a simple cold. Understanding the folk terminology can assist responders in understanding patient needs.

Responders can offer assistance that "complements" the treatments of Curanderismo. However, responders may find it challenging to offer comfort and protection from magical sicknesses, such as Mal de Ojo. The responder should allow the patient to hold whatever objects of protection to feel comfort in his/her spiritual worldview. As always, if a responder does not subscribe to the patient's beliefs system, he should still treat the patient and patient's worldview with respect.

Methods of Healing

Curanderismo provides a holistic approach to healing that incorporates the emotional, mental and physical body. Healing may come from a ritual or from a prescription from a Curandero or even possibly a remedy that is taught by members of the community. The Remedios Caseros (or home remedy) may be something as basic as a bowl of soup or an herbal tea.

The Curandero relies on a number of ritualistic practices in provident treatment of his clients. One of the most common rituals involves the use of an object to "sweep" away sickness. The Baridda (or sweeping) may involve herbs, lemons, eggs or flowers. These objects may be passed over the body of the client to rid him/her of negative influences, called Vibraciones Malos, that are causing sickness. The objects may also be used to sweep positive influences over the infected individual, called Vibraciones Positivas. Prayers are spoken over the individual during the sweeping, which can include the Lord's Prayer and the Apostles Creed. A ritual cleansing (or Limpiza) may use an egg or an animal passed over the body of the client to "clean" them of a sickness. The animal may be killed, but the egg is traditionally placed in a glass under the client's bed. If by morning, the egg has become cooked or bloody, it has been successful in taking away the illness.

A ritual using incense to "cleanse" a home or business may be used by the Curandero provident. The Sahumerio is a ritual cleansing of an environment by waving the smoke from the incense into a specified space. The ritual Sortilegio involves the use of objects to "tie up" negative influences that may affect a client. Ribbons and cords may be used to tie up artifacts. The Curandero may also use candles in the diagnosis of sickness. The pattern in which the flame moves or in which the wax burns may provide the healer with spiritual insight into the client's illness.

Objects may be used to transfer the sickness into a vessel. The treatment of folk illnesses, such as Insolacion, may involve a glass of water being placed above the client's head. When the water boils, the sickness has been removed. The treatment of stomach problems may be treated with the application to the stomach of alcohol-soaked bread and herbs.

Herbalism

The use of medicinal herbs (Plantas Medicinales) to heal is a primary healing technique used by the Curandero. The specialized knowledge of herbs used by the healer does not only recognize the medicinal purposes of herb, but also the magical properties of herbs. As in many religious cultures, herbs are recognized as living objects that contain energy and vibrations. These energies can provide healing for the human body. Herbs are used in home remedies known as Remedios Caseros. Herbs may be used in a raw form, teas, powders, oils and even soaps (Figure 7.8). The following are some examples of herbs and their uses in Curanderismo.

Figure 7.8 Patients may use herbal soaps and oils designed to physically and spiritually heal aches and pains.

Chamomile (Manzanilla): Susto, Mal de Ojo
Borraja: Bladder, infection
Sage Plant: Formed in shape of a cross and placed under a pillow
Cactus (Nopal): Diabetes
Altamisa (Mountain Mugwort): Colds and flu
Brook Mint (Poleo): Fever and headaches
Spearmint (Yerba Buena): Nervousness
Orange Leaves (Te De Nurranjo): Nervousness, acts as a sedative
Sweet Basil (Albacar): Wards off evil spirits

Objects of Healing

There are a number of objects used in healing as well as for luck and protection. Patients who wear or display these objects should be allowed to keep them unless the object is threatening the health of the patient. Many healing objects appear to be very mundane, but they do provide personal comfort to the patient. Beans, beads, necklaces and herbal amulets may be worn by the patient (Figure 7.9). Many objects of healing and protection will be decorated with images of saints and important spiritual personalities. Some of the widely used objects and their descriptions are as follows:

Horseshoe Amulet

The horseshoe is an object of luck. Patients may have a horseshoe made of garlic above the door of their home or business. The garlic keeps away evil. Horseshoes may be found in a miniature form on necklaces, bracelets and amulet bags. One amulet is found in the form of a shadowbox frame that contains a horseshoe, an image of Saint Martin de Cabellero, beads, coins and beans.

Figure 7.9 Patients may wear necklaces dedicated to folk saints. This necklace is used for protection and depicts Our Lady of Guadalupe and the bandit Jesus Malverde.

Lodestone

The lodestone, called Piedra Iman, is used as an amulet in a number of forms. The stone contains magnetic properties that are said to "pull" or attract positive desires. The stone may be placed in a small bag and "fed" magnetic particles to make it grow in size. Lodestone may be placed in a bag along with beads, coins, beans and a horseshoe. These amulets provide protection of health, family and success.

Scapulario

The Scapular is a cloth worn by Catholics that displays an image of a saint. Followers of Curandrismo may wear images of the folk saint, such as Santa Muerte.

Milagro

The Milagro (or Miracle) is a miniature body part that is used to represent the appendage that is in need of healing, The Milagro may be found placed on images of saints to bring about healing.

La Manito de Coral

This black image of a hand represents the "hand of God."

Ojo de Venado

Also known as Deer's Eye (Figure 7.10). This is one of the more widely available amulets available at various Latin markets throughout the United States. The object provides protection from the Mal de Ojo (or Evil Eye) (Figure 7.10). The

Figure 7.10 The Ojo De Vando or Deer's Eye is used to ward off the evil eye or Mal de Ojo. Responders should allow patients to wear amulets such as this if the patient feels it necessary.

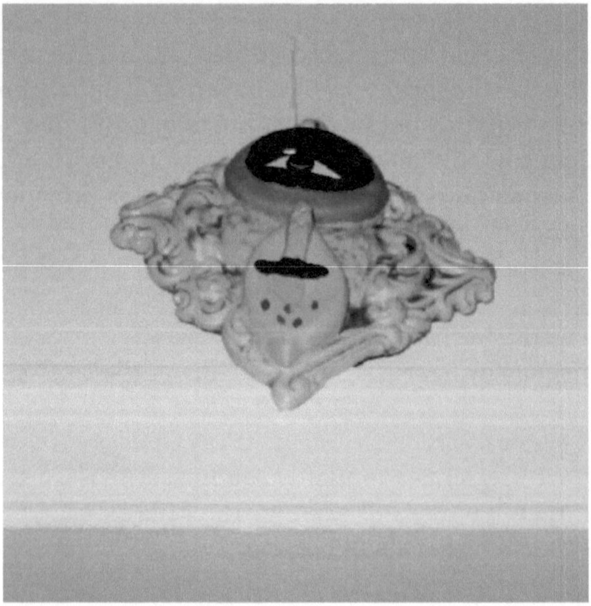

Figure 7.11 An amulet used to ward off the evil eye. Responders may encounter amulets hanging above doorways when responding to calls.

amulet is a velvet bean, also known as a buckeye, wrapped in red cord (Figure 7.11). The bean may have an image of a saint decorated on it. There are several variations of the Ojo De Venado. Some include the Manito de Coral or Hand of God in the amulet.

Responder Issues

Responders may find that practitioners want to use folk healing remedies alongside the treatment that responders are trying to provide. Allow the patient to use their cultural remedy if it does not create a hazard in providing treatment. If the remedy or ritual is taking time that is necessary to provide emergency treatment, advise the patient in a respectful and patient manner of the urgency.

Dr. Antonio N. Zavaleta[4] points out that many chronic ailments, such as diabetes and arthritis, go untreated in the Mexican American community. For this reason, it's essential that folk healers be networked with medical professionals. However, Dr. Zavaleta also cautions that not all healers are reputable and some can cause a great deal of harm.

Responders assessing scenes may discover that smoke from burning incense is creating a hazard for the patient. If necessary, ask the patient or

Figure 7.12 The Curandero is the local healer, psychiatrist and priest. Through the use of herbs, candles and the spiritual realm, the Curandero provides treatment to those in the Latin community.

any others present to extinguish the incense. Responders may also be advised that incense in a poorly ventilated environment cause health problems.

Responders may discover that the patient has ingested herbal remedies. If herbs are present, they may not be properly labeled. Responders may find the folk name of herbs on bottles and bags. Ask the patient if you may take the herbs with you for identification purposes. Herb names may appear according to their folk name, their botanical name, in Spanish and in English. Some herbal remedies may contain lead and can cause illness.

Some Curanderos (Figure 7.12) have suggested to clients seeking an abortion to use Rue or Ruda. Rue is a traditional abortifacient (causing abortion). Rue stimulates the uterus and nervous system. Rue can irritate kidneys and cause liver degeneration.

One folk treatment for Fallen Fontanelle is having an adult suck on the anterior fontanelle. This sucking can cause bruising on the head. The child may also be held upside down for one minute while the child's feet are tapped three times. Some responders have observed that the sunken fontenelle may be a symptom of dehydration.

Patients who consult Curanderos and receive directions to use herbal treatments may not be given exact dosage information. An overdose of an herb could result in sickness or even death.

Some healers do cross the border into the United States to perform services for patients. Responders may discover hesitancy from patients to discuss their healer if the healer is in the United States without proper authorization.

Reference

1. Spielberg, Joseph and Zavaleta, Antonio. Historic Folk Sainthood along the Texas-Mexico Border, Research Project and Web site at: http://www.vpea.utb.edu/elnino/researcharticles/historicfolksainthood.html
2. Handbook of Texas Online: Web site at: http://www.tsha.utexas.edu/handbook/online/articles/CC/sdc1.html
3. Torres, Eliseo. *The Folk Healer: The Mexican Tradition of Curanderismo*. Albuquerque, NM: Nieves Press, 1985.
4. Zavaleta, Antonio N., "Do cultural factors affect Hispanic health status?" Proceedings of the Rio Grande Valley Public Health Community Conference, Rio Grand Valley, TX sponsored by UTHSC–School of Public Health, June 8,2000.

8 Closing Issues

Behavior

In order to assess if the patient views an illness as spiritual in nature, responders should watch for references to gods or spirits. Patients who use religious objects may be using them as protection from spiritual harm. Prayer and chanting may also be an indication that the patient believes an illness is spiritual in nature.

Language

Realize that language may also present an additional factor in communicating with patients of various nationalities. Members may require the use of translators in order to effectively communicate needs and issues.

Patience

Understand that cultures respond to stresses in different ways.

Communication

Ask questions slowly and one at a time.

Determine what religious aspects are important to the patient and determine a common goal for you and the patient. Stress that your goal is not to disturb the religious practices used in healing, but that you are there to "complement" these practices.[1]

Realize that fear of authority may create an obstacle in communicating with your patient. A patient who may use bizarre or even illegal practices in observing religious traditions may be scared to communicate with authorities for fear of being arrested. Some patients may fear that responders may not understand the practices and customs of a religion and will treat them differently. It is important that as a responder you convey a sense of concern for the patient's health despite the religious preferences of the patient.

It is understandable that rituals and artifacts of a religious culture may appear intimidating to responders who have never encountered them before. Even if your personal outlook on these items is one of, perhaps, fear, you should remain focused on the task of assisting the patients and creating a safe environment for them and yourself. Do not show shock or offense in front of a patient when encountering these items.

In the healthcare field, a popular approach to other cultures is found in a strategy known as "Kleinman's Tool to Elicit Health Beliefs in Clinical Encounters."[2] The following are questions used in assessing the cultural attitude toward health from the patient's worldview.

1. What do you call your problem? What name does it have?
2. What do you think caused your problem?
3. Why do you think it started when it did?
4. What does your sickness do to you? How does it work?
5. How severe is it? Will it have a short or long course?
6. What do you fear most about your disorder?
7. What are the chief problems that your sickness has caused for you?
8. What kind of treatment do you think you should receive?
9. What are the important results you hope to receive from treatment?

Generalizations

Some of the artifacts and rituals in many of the African traditional religions may appear similar, but are very different. A responder that refers to a Santeria altar as Voodoo in the presence of a patient may find that the patient is offended by this misidentifying of a culture. Before risking offending a patient, ask them about their culture.

It's also important to remember that ideal norms of conduct may differ from the actual behavior of the practitioner you encounter.

References

1. Andrews, Margaret M. *Transcultural Concepts in Nursing Care,* Scott, Foresman and Company, Glenview, IL, 1989, chap. 13.
2. Kleinman, Arthur. Kleinman's tool to elicit health beliefs in clinical encounters, in *Patients and Healers in the Context of Culture.* University of California Press, Berkeley, CA, 1981.

Glossary of Cultural Terms

Responders may discover terms used by member of various magico-religious faiths that are used only within the specific religious cultures. The following is a glossary of commonly used terms in the magico-religious communities (*religious cultures are in italics*).

Addimu *(Regla de Ocha)* A lesser offering in Santeria. Usually consists of fruits and nonblood-containing items.

Akasha *(Wicca)* Term used to describe the spirit.

Akashic Records *(Wicca)* A library of records of past events and memories of every human being.

Aleyo *(Regla de Ocha)* A noninitiate to Santeria. Literally means "stranger" or outsider.

Ashe *(Regla de Ocha)* Term used to describe the "magic" of the Orishas in Santeria. Ache is divine energy.

Asiento *(Regla de Ocha)* "Making the Saint" in Santeria. Asiento is the term used to describe placing or "seating" of the Orisha into the head of the initiate.

Aspects *(Wicca)* Term used to describe the qualities of a deity. For example, Hecate is an aspect of the goddess.

Asson *(Voodoo)* A rattle used in Voodoo by initiated clergy. Typically covered in beads or snake bones.

Baba *(Regla de Ocha)* Term meaning Father.

Babalawo *(Regla de Ocha)* He is the Father of the Secrets. The term is used to denote the high priest in Santeria that can use the Table of Ifa divination system.

Babalocha *(Regla de Ocha)* Term used to denote the male initiate in Santeria.

Baka *(Voodoo)* Dwarf-like spirit invoked by a Voodoo priest for protection.

Banish *(Wicca)* The act of driving away negative energy or spirits.

Bata *(Regla de Ocha)* Sacred drums used in Santeria ceremonies.

Bembe *(Regla de Ocha)* Ritual party for the Orishas of Santeria.

Billis *(Curanderismo)* Illness caused by suppressed anger.

Bilongo *(Regla de Ocha and Las Reglas de Congo)* A spell or medicine, usually found in the form of a "bundle."

Bind *(Wicca)* Term used to describe a magical action that stops someone from performing an action, such as abuse, theft or harm.

Bosal *(Voodoo)* Term meaning "wild" or "untamed" Refers to an initiate who has not learned to work with spirits.

Boveda *(Regla de Ocha)* The altar used to honor the Eggun (ancestors).

Brujeria *(Curanderismo/Regla de Ocha)* Term used to describe malevolent sorcery.

BTW *(Wicca)* Nickname for British traditional witchcraft, which is a term used to describe a number of Wiccan traditions that originated in the New Forest region of England.

Cantos *(Regla de Ocha)* Song used to praise the Orishas.

Centering *(Wicca)* Making oneself balanced and mentally focused.

Chamalongo *(Las Reglas de Congo)* Divination system using coconut shells to interact with the spirits.

Cone of Power *(Wicca)* Term used to describe the energy that is raised during a Wiccan ritual.

Coven *(Wicca)* An assembly of witches.

Cowan *(Wicca)* Term used to denote a non-Wiccan.

Craft, the *(Wicca)* Term used to describe the activities and beliefs of witches.

Cuchillo *(Regla de Ocha)* The knife used to make sacrifices in Santeria.

Curandera *(Curanderismo)* The traditional title for a female healer.

Curandero *(Curanderismo)* The traditional title for a male healer.

Darle Coco El Santo *(Regla de Ocha)* Divination system using the coconut.

Deosil *(Wicca)* A term used to describe moving clockwise around a circle during a ritual.

Despojo *(Regla de Ocha)* A cleansing ceremony in Santeria.

Diloggun *(Regla de Ocha)* Divination system using the cowrie shells.

Don *(Curanderismo)* A gift from God.

Ebbo *(Regla de Ocha)* A major sacrifice in Santeria. The blood from animals is typically used to receive Ache from the Orishas.

Eggun *(Regla de Ocha/Las Reglas de Congo)* Term used to describe the dead or ancestors. The Eggun are honored in rituals and through the altars known as Boveda.

Elementals *(Wicca)* Personifications of the elements of Earth, Wind, Water and Fire.

Empacho *(Curanderismo)* Illness caused by food lodged in the digestive tract.

Esbat *(Wicca)* Term used to denote the meetings held according to the changing phases of the moon. Some covens meet only on days of the full moon.

Ewe *(Regla de Ocha)* The Ewe are the herbs and plants used in Santeria.

Fam-Trad *(Wicca)* Term used to describe Family Traditions of witchcraft.

Firma *(Las Reglas de Congo)* The signatures of the spirits in Kongo religions. The firma are typically drawn to invoke the spiritual presence of a deity.

Fula *(Las Reglas de Congo)* Gunpowder used in Congo-based rituals.

Garde *(Voodoo)* A ritual scarring in which magical protection is placed on an individual.

Gros-Bon-Ange *(Voodoo)* The "big guardian angel" that is part of man. The term refers to the psyche of humanity.

Grounding *(Wicca)* Term used to describe the release of excess energy at the end of a ritual.

Guerreros *(Regla de Ocha)* The warrior Orishas of Santeria, they include Eleggua, Oggun and Ochosi. Osun is also received with these Orishas.

Idé *(Regla de Ocha)* The beaded bracelet that is owned by Orun. The bracelet is colored yellow and green and protects the owner from death.

Ifa *(Regla de Ocha)* Ifa is a West African system of divination. It also means "fate."

Iku *(Regla de Ocha)* The spirit of death.

Ile *(Regla de Ocha)* Term used to mean house. The ile is the fellowship of practitioners.

Iya *(Regla de Ocha)* Iya is known as the "mother" of the sacred Bata drums used in ceremonies.

Iyalocha *(Regla de Ocha)* Term used to denote female initiates in Santeria.

Iyawo *(Regla de Ocha)* The initiate in Santeria. Iyawo means the "bride" of the Orisha.

Kariocha *(Regla de Ocha)* The ceremony in which the initiate becomes a priest/priestess.

Karma *(Wicca)* A concept from Eastern religion referring to the good or evil deeds that a person may commit and the result of these deeds.

Lady *(Wicca)* Term of respect for a High Priestess.

La Place *(Voodoo)* Master of ceremonies at a Voodoo ritual.

Lave-tet *(Voodoo)* Head washing ceremony.

Loa *(Voodoo)* The deities or spirits of Voodoo.

Los Tres Grandes *(Curanderismo)* Term used to refer to the Three Great Healers: El Nino Findenco, Don Pedrito Jaramillo and Teresita.

Lucumi *(Regla de Ocha)* Term describing the Yoruba people in Cuba.

Macuto *(Regla de Ocha/Las Reglas de Congo)* Amulet filled with herbs and Ache.

Malferefun *(Regla de Ocha)* Lucumi term for "praised be."

Mal de Ojo *(Curanderismo)* The illness known as the Evil Eye.

Mal Dyok (Maldjok) *(Voodoo)* The term used to denote the Evil Eye in the Haitian community.

Mambo *(Las Reglas de Congo/Voodoo)* In Kongo religions, the Mambo is a song used to invoke a spirit. In Voodoo, the Mambo is the priestess of the religion.

Menga *(Las Reglas de Congo)* Menga means "blood" in the Kikongo language. Animal blood is offered to the Nganga in the Kongo religions.

Moyuba *(Regla de Ocha)* An invocational prayer in Santeria.

Mpungo *(Las Reglas de Congo)* The Bantu deities in Palo Mayombe and other Kongo traditions.

Nganga *(Las Reglas de Congo)* A term originally used to describe the healer in West African Bantu religions. It is used in contemporary practices to describe the sacred vessel that houses the spirits. The Nganga is usually an iron cauldron or a ceramic pot.

Nkisi *(Las Reglas de Congo)* The term used to originally describe the sacred medicines and bundles used by Bantu priests. The Nkisi is used to denote the material object that houses the spirits of the dead.

Nkobos *(Las Reglas de Congo)* Divination system using seashells.

Obi *(Regla de Ocha)* The coconut oracle used in Santeria.

Orishas *(Regla de Ocha)* The deities of Santeria.

Otan *(Regla de Ocha)* The sacred stone that contains the essence of the Orisha.

Padrino *(Regla de Ocha)* Term used to describe the spiritual godfather who initiates a believer.

Palero/Palera *(Las Reglas de Congo)* The office of priest or priestess in Palo Mayombe and Kongo faiths.

Palo Christianos *(Las Reglas de Congo)* A term used to describe those practitioners who dedicate their vessels to the benevolent deity Nzambi.

Palo Judias *(Las Reglas de Congo)* A term used to describe those practitioners who dedicate their vessels to Kadiempembe or Lukankasi, which has been interpreted by some as the devil.

Partera *(Curanderismo)* Healer who serves as a midwife.

Pataki *(Las Reglas de Congo)* The myths and legends used to communicate the rituals and beliefs of the Orishas.

Piedra Iman *(Curanderismo)* A lodestone used in magical workings to attract positive energies.

Poteau-Mitan *(Voodoo)* The pole in the center of the temple used to call Voodoo spirits.

Prenda *(Las Reglas de Congo)* A term that means jewel. It is used to refer to the Nganga.

Rama *(Las Reglas de Congo)* The traditions or "branches" of the Kongo religions.

Rayado *(Las Reglas de Congo)* The ritual in which an initiate makes a pact with the spirits. Rayado means *consecrated* and refers to the cutting ceremony. Also known as being "scratched in."

Recetas *(Curanderismo)* The prescriptions given by the healer.

Resguardo *(Las Reglas de Congo)* A charm used to protect.

Sabbat *(Wicca)* The sacred days that honor the eight festivals celebrating the change in seasons.

Sahumerio *(Curanderismo)* A ritual in which incense is used to send away negative energies.

Skyclad *(Wicca)* A term used to describe ritual nudity.

Sobador *(Curanderismo)* A healer who uses massage techniques for healing.

Susto *(Curanderismo)* Shock or loss of spirit due to trauma.

Tambor *(Regla de Ocha)* A ceremony in which the sacred drums are played.

Tata *(Las Reglas de Congo)* A term used to mean Father. Used to describe an office of initiation in Palo Mayombe.

Ti-Bon-Ange (Ti-Bon-Anj) *(Voodoo)* The "little guardian angel" that composes the soul. The angel is compared to consciousness.

Voodon Original term used for "spirit" that later became voodoo. Voodon is a term used many times to describe a voodoo-type aspect and is used interchangeably with voodoo.

Wanga *(Voodoo)* Charm used for malevolent workings.

Watchtower *(Wicca)* The term used to describe the elements and their direction. The Guardians of the Watchtower are called to protect the ritual space during the ceremony.

Widdershins *(Wicca)* Ritual action of moving counterclockwise in a circle. Used to get rid of energy.

Yerbero *(Curanderismo)* Title used by healers who use herbal treatments.

Index of Symbols

The following are some of the images that responders may discover during calls involving magico-religious groups.

Symbols of Asatru

Odin's Rune: One of the letters in the Runic alphabet. Associated with the deity Odin.

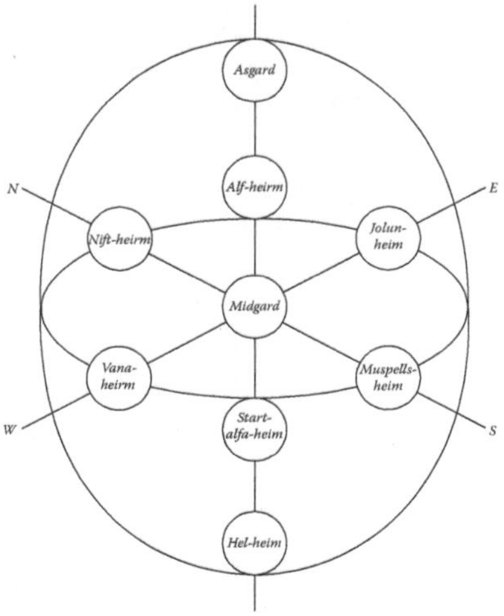

Nine Worlds: Image representing the cosmology or universe of the Asatru.

Valknot: Also known as Knot of the Slain. Used for protective purposes.

Tyr Rune: Rune representing the deity Tyr, the god of war and heroic glory.

Thor's Hammer: Also known as Mjolnir. Represents the tool of the deity Thor.

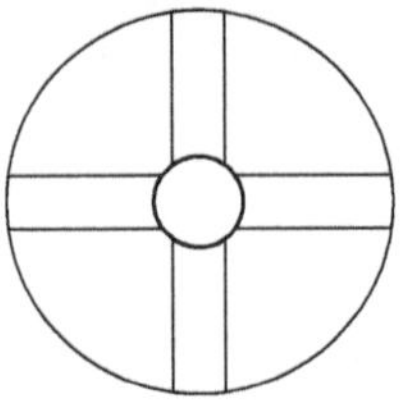

Solar Cross: An ancient symbol used to represent the movement of the sun.

Symbols of Voodoo

Agwe: The Loa representing nature and the woods.

Ogou: The god of metal and iron.

Legba: The Loa that opens the crossroads and fate.

Dambalah: The Loa that purifies initiates; rules the marketplace.

Erzulie: Loa of the dead (Ghede).

Gran Bois: Wife of Baron Samedi. She protects gravestones.

Symbols of Wicca

Pentagram: Image that represents the elements subdued by spirits.

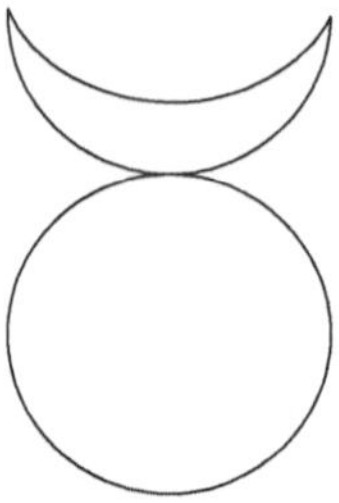

Horned God: Image representing the male aspect of deity.

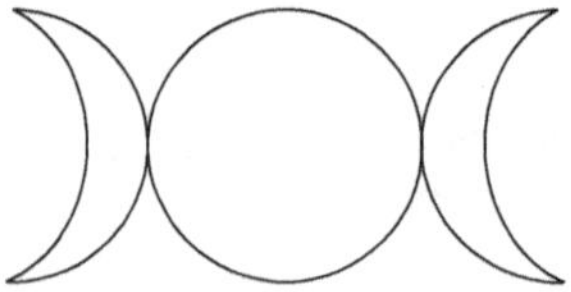

Triple Goddess: Image representing the maiden, mother and crone phases of the goddess.

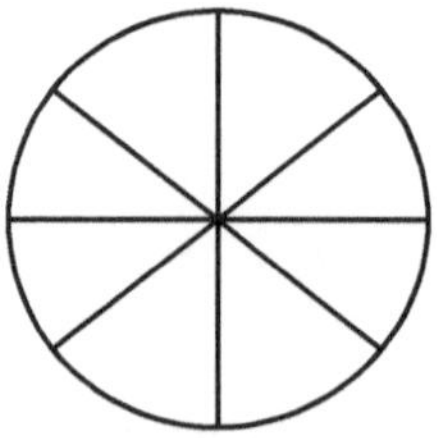

Wheel of the Year: An Egyptian symbol of life and rebirth.

Labrys: A symbol that represents the female element.

Lambrynth: Also known as the Triskele, the image represents several different concepts, including the goddess and the Trinity of Christianity.

Symbols of Palo Mayombe and other Kongo Religious Cultures

Lucero: The signature or Firma used to invoke the Mpungu that opens the spiritual realm.

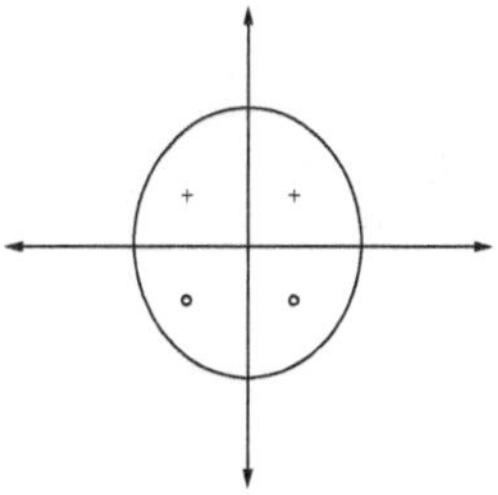

Zarabanda: The firma used to invoke the Mpungu over iron and war.

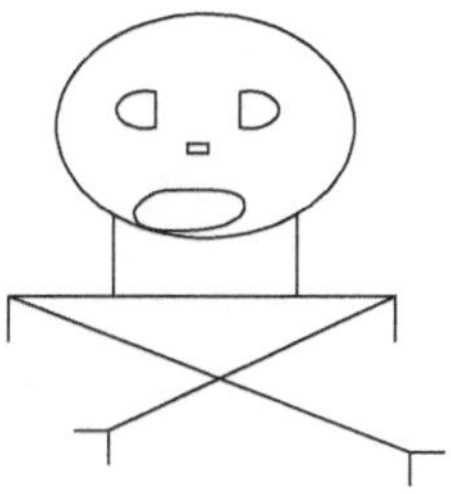

Nfumbe: A symbol used in rituals involving the spirits of the dead.

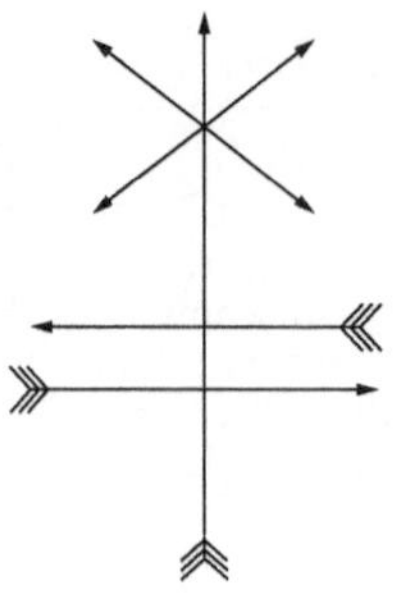

Fula: A symbol used in rituals while using Fula (gunpowder).

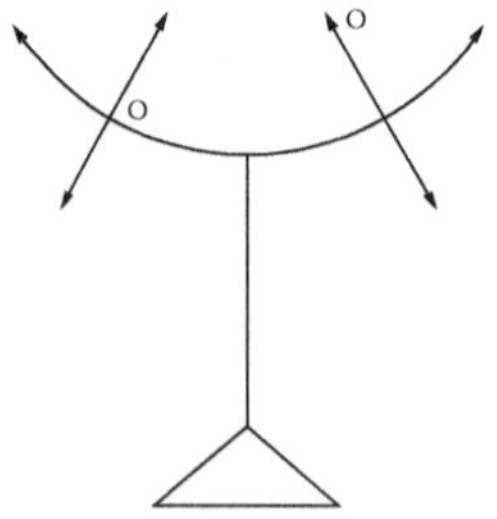

Mother Kengue: A symbol used to represent an aspect of Tiembla Tierra, the Mpungu that rules hills and mountains.

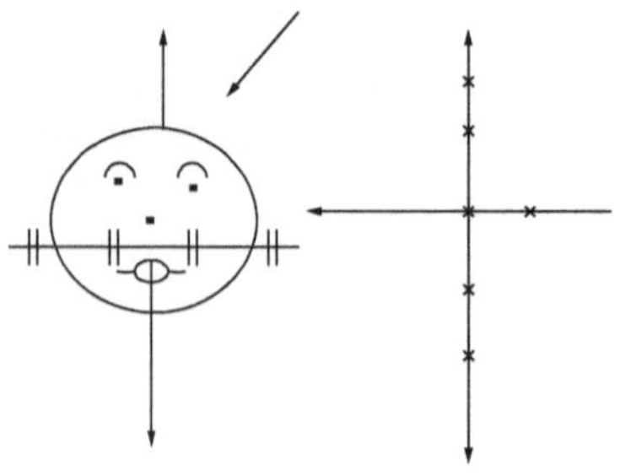

Magical Working: An example of a drawing used in ritual work.

Subject Index

A

Account of evil, 8
Addimu, 56–57, 131
Aganyu, 47–48, 63
Agassou, 92
Aggayu, 58
Agwe, 93, 101, 104, 128
Akasha, 131
Akasha records, 131
Albacar, 120
Alexandrian Wicca, 16, 19
Aleyo, 49, 131
Altamisa, 120
Amulet(s), 36
  handling of, 68
  herbal, 120
  horseshoe, 120
  mercury in, 66
  for patient comfort, 86, 121
Ancestor reverence, 48–49
Angelica, 32
Animal sacrifices, 42, 45, 57–58, 81
Anise, 65
Arabic gum, 33
Aromatherapy, 29
Artemis herb, 33
Artifacts, 9
Asatru, 14, 127
Ashe, 131
Asiento, 53, 61, 131
Aspects, 131
Asson, 96–97, 131
Athame, 20
Atipola, 65
Auric healing, 29–30
Awe, 8
Ayido Wedo, 92, 101
Ayizan, 91
Azaka, 92, 101, 104

B

Baba, 131
Babalawo, 42, 47, 50, 131
Babalocha, 50, 132
Babalu-Aye, 46
  animal sacrifice for, 58
  celebration day, 61
  divine punishment, 63
  necklace, 51
  offering to, 57
Baka, 105, 132
Banishment, 24, 132
Bantu, 71–73. *See also* Palo Mayombe
  religious elements, 72–73
  traditions, 71–72
Baron Lao, 104
Baron Samedi, 94, 101
Basil, 33, 65, 120
Bata, 132
Belief in supernatural beings, 7
Bell, 20
Bembe, 61, 132
Benzoin, 33
Billis, 118, 132
Bilongo, 132
Bind, 132
Boliene, 20
Bones, 75–76
Book of Shadows, 20
Borraja, 120
Bosal, 132
Bottles, 97
Boveda, 49, 60, 132
Brilumba, 71
British Traditional Wicca (BTW), 16, 132
Brook mint, 120
Brujeria, 60, 62, 116, 132
BTW. *See* British Traditional Wicca (BTW)

C

Cactus, 120
Caida de Mollera, 117
Camphor, 65
Candles, magic, 35
Cano brava, 76
Cantos, 132
Carbonero, 85
Carrefour, 93
Cauldron, 27
Ceiba tree, 86
Celtic Wicca, 16
Censer, 20
Centelle Ndoki, 74
  sacred vessel, 79
Centering, 132
Cereke, 85
Ceremonies, 21
Chakras, 31
  crown, 31
  heart, 31
  navel, 31
  root, 31
  solar plexus, 31
  third eye, 31
  throat, 31
Chalice, 20
Chamalongo, 81, 82, 132
Chamba, 84, 85
Chamomile, 33, 65, 120
Chango, 45
  animal sacrifice for, 58
  celebration day, 61
  divine punishment, 63
  father, 48
  necklace, 51
  offering, 57
  sons, 47
Chanting, 29
Choya Wengue, 74
Chromolithograph, 97
Circle, 19
Common nettle, 33
Conch shell, 98
Cone of Power, 24, 132
Cord healing, 29
Cords, 21
Corobane, 32–33
Correspondences, 21–22
  color, 22
Corta Lima, 71
Coven, 19, 20, 132
Cowan, 132
Craft, 37, 132
Cuchillo, 132
Cultural competency, 4, 7–8
Curandera, 115, 116, 132
Curanderismo, 109–124
  beliefs and practices, 109–115
  folk saints, 109–115
    Dr. Jose Gregorio Hernandez, 113
    Jesus Malverde, 113
    Juan Soldado, 113
    Judas Tudeo, 112
    Our Lady of Guadalupe, 110–111
    San Martin Caballero, 111, 112
    San Martin de Porres, 111
    San Simon, 113
    San Toribio Romo, 113
    Santa Marta, 113
    Santa Muerte, 114
  group structure, 115–116
  healing and sickness, 117–122
  herbalism, 119–120
  illnesses, 117–118
    Billis, 118
    Caida de Mollera, 117
    Empacho, 117
    Encono, 117
    Insolacion, 118
    Mal Aire, 117
    Mal de Latido, 118
    Mal de Ojo, 117
    Malificia, 117
    Melarchico, 117
    Sangre Debil, 118
    Susto, 117
  methods of healing, 118–120
  objects of healing, 120–122
    horseshoe amulet, 120
    La Manito de Coral, 121
    Lodestone, 121
    Milagro, 121
    Ojo de Venado, 121–122
    Scapulario, 121
  responder issues, 122–123
Curandero, 115, 132
Cursed objects, 37

D

Damballah Wedo, 92, 101, 128
Darle Coco El Santo, 54, 133
Deadly nightshade, 32
Deities, 9
Deosil, 22, 133
Despojo, 64, 133
Devil's apple, 32
Dianic Wicca, 16
Diloggun, 56, 133
Dominican Voodoo, 106
Don, 133
Dr. Jose Gregorio Hernandez, 113
Druidism, 14
Drums
  Congo, 98
  Petro, 98
  Rada, 98
  Voodoo
    Congo, 98
    Petro, 98
    Rada, 98

E

Ebbo, 57–58, 133
Eclectic Wicca, 16
Eggun, 48–49, 133
Elegua, 43–44
  animal sacrifice for, 58
  celebration day, 61
  divine punishment, 63
  necklace, 51
  offering to, 56
Elementals, 7, 24, 133
Elements, 27
Empacho, 2, 109, 117, 133
Encono, 117
Erzulie Dantor, 94, 128
Esbat, 25, 133
Espanta Muerto, 85
Espartillo, 65
Ewe, 133
Ezili Danto, 94, 101, 104
Ezili Freda, 92, 104

F

Fam-Trad, 133
Fennel, 33
Firma, 77, 78, 83, 84, 130, 133
First responder issues. *See also* Responder issues
  Curanderismo, 122–123
  harmful implements, 39
  in Palo Mayombe, 86–87
  in Santeria, 67–68
  in Voodooism, 107–108
  weapons, 39
  in Wiccan religion, 38–39
Flags, 97
Francisco and Francisca, 80
Frankincense, 33
Fula, 81, 84, 130, 133

G

Garde, 101, 105, 108, 133
Garden Angelica, 32
Garden thyme, 32
Gardenarian Wicca, 16–17
Gede, 94, 101, 104
Georgian Wicca, 17
Glossary, 131–136
Gran Bwa, 93, 129
Greater nettle, 33
Gros-Bon-Ange, 133
Ground apple, 33
Grounding, 22, 31, 133
Group structure, 19–20
  circle, 19
  coven, 19, 20
  Curanderismo, 115–116
  grove, 19
  order, 19
  Palo Mayombe, 80–81
  Santeria, 49–50
  Voodoo, 95–96
  Wiccan religion, 19–20
Grove, 19
Guerreros, 52, 133
Gurufinda, 74

H

Harmful implements, 39
Hemlock, 32–33
Herb Bennet, 32–33
Herb of Circe, 32
Herb of grace, 33

Herbalism
- Curanderismo, 119–120
- Palo Mayombe, 84–85
- Santeria, 64–65
- in Wiccan religion, 31–33

Hereditary Wicca, 17
Hogweed, 65
Horned God, 129
Horseshoe amulet, 120

I

Ibeji, 47, 61
Idé, 66, 133
Ifa, 47, 50, 134
Iku, 52, 66, 134
Ile, 134
Inkita, 85
Inle, 48
- celebration day, 61
- divine punishment, 63
- offering to, 57

Insolacion, 118
Institutionalized sharing, 8
Iya, 134
Iyalocha, 51, 134
Iyawo, 61, 134

J

Jesus Malverde, 113, 120
Jewelry, 36–37
Juan Soldado, 113
Judas Tudeo, 112
Juno's tears, 33

K

Kalfu, 93
Kalunga, 75
Kariocha, 9, 53–54, 134
Karma, 18, 134
Kimbisa, 71
Kobayende, 74

L

La Manito de Coral, 121, 122
La Place, 98, 134
La Sirene, 92, 104
Labrys, 129
Lady, 134
Lambrynth, 129
Lave-tet, 134
Law of Contact, 10, 11
Legba, 90, 101, 104, 128
Loa(s), 7, 90, 134
- Agassou, 92
- Agwe, 93
- Ayida Wedo, 92
- Ayizan, 91
- Azaka, 92
- Baron Samedi, 94
- Carrefour, 93
- Damballah Wedo, 92
- Erzulie Dantor, 94
- Ezili Danto, 94
- Ezili Freda, 92
- Gede, 94
- Gran Bwa, 93
- Kalfu, 93
- La Sirene, 92
- Loko, 91
- Mama Brigette, 95
- Marasa, 90
- Marinette-Bwa-Chech, 94
- Ogou Group, 93
- Petro, 93
- Rada, 90
- Simbi, 93, 94
- Sobo, 92
- Ti-Jean Petro, 94

Lodestone, 121
Loko, 91
Los Tres Grandes, 114, 134
Lucero, 74, 79, 130
- sacred vessel, 78

Lucumi, 42, 53, 58, 61, 134

M

Macuto, 66, 134
Madre de Agua, 75
- sacred vessel, 80

Magic
- practices, 10
- in religious culture (*See* Magico-religious culture(s))

Magical Working, 11, 130, 135
Magico-religious culture(s), 10–11

worldview, 10
Mal Aire, 117
Mal de Latido, 118
Mal de Ojo, 8, 9, 117, 118, 120, 121, 134
Mal djok, 105, 134
Mal Dyok, 105, 134
Malferefun, 134
Malificia, 117
Mama Chola, 74
Mama Kengue, 74, 130
Mama Nsasi, 74
Mama Sholan, 78
Maman Brigette, 95
Mambo, 81, 82
Voodoo, 94, 95, 96, 97, 106, 108, 134
Mandrake, 32
Manzanilla, 65, 120
Marasa, 90
Maravilla, 65
Marinette-Bwa-Chech, 94
Mariwanga, 74
Marjoram, 65
Masterwort, 32
Mecheiso, 85
Mejorana, 65
Melarchico, 117
Menga, 79, 81, 134
Mercury, ritualistic use, 66, 87
Milagro, 121
Mohsian tradition Wiccan religion, 17
Moral code, 7
Mountain mugwort, 120
Moyuba, 58, 134
Mpungo (Spirits of nature), 74, 75, 80, 135
Centelle Ndoki, 74
Choya Wengue, 74
Gurufinda, 74
Kalunga, 75
Kobayende, 74
Lucero, 74
Madre de Agua, 75
Mama Chola, 74
Mama Kengue, 74, 130
Mama Nsasi, 74
Mariwanga, 74
Siete Rayos, 74
Tata Nfumbe, 74, 130
Tiembla Tierra, 74
Zarabanda, 75, 78, 81, 130
Mugwort, 33
Mysticism, 8
Myth, 9

N

Naughty man, 33
Neopaganism, 13–39
religions of, 14–15
Nettle, 33
New Orleans Voodoo, 106–107
Nganga, 2, 72, 73, 83, 135
bones in, 75
horn in transporting materials from, 85
in initiation, 83
responder responsibility when finding, 86
spaces for, 76, 77
Nine Worlds, 127
Nkisi, 72, 74, 135
Nkobos, 135
Nopal, 120
Nzambi, 73, 74, 135

O

Obatala, 45, 63
animal sacrifice for, 58
celebration day, 61
divine punishment, 63
offering to, 57
Obi, 54–55, 135
Oblibanum, 33
Ochosi, 45, 57, 61
Odin's Rune, 127
Offerings, 27
Santeria gods, 57
Ogan, 98
Ogou group, 93, 101, 104, 128
Ogun, 45
animal sacrifice for, 58
celebration day, 61
divine punishment, 63
necklace, 51
Oko, 48
Olokun, 46, 63
Orange Leaves, 120
Order, 19
Orishas, 74, 75, 131, 132, 133, 134, 135
Orula/Orunmila, 47
celebration day, 61
necklace, 51
punishment, 63
Osain, 47, 63, 64
Oshun, 45, 47

animal sacrifice for, 58
celebration day, 61
divine punishment, 63
necklace, 51
offering to, 57
Otan, 53, 54, 135
Our Lady of Guadalupe, 110–111
Oya, 45–46
celebration day, 61
offering to, 57

P

Packets, 98
Padrino, 50, 135
Palero/Palera, 77, 80, 85, 135
Palo Christianos, 74, 135
Palo Judias, 135
Palo Mayombe, 71–87
articles of comfort, 85–86
beliefs and practices, 73–75
bones in, 75–76
cano brava in, 76
Ceiba tree and, 86
Chamba, 84, 85
divination, 81
group structure, 80–81
healing and sickness, 85–86
Herbalism, 84–85
initiation, 82–84
Mpungo as spirits of nature, 74–75 (*See also* Mpungo)
Nzambi as creator, 73
responder issues, 86–87
rituals and ceremonies, 81
Rogación de Cabeza, 86
sacred spaces, 76–77
sacrifices, 81–82
symbols, 130
Fula, 130
Lucero, 130
Magical Working, 130
Mother Kengue, 130
Nfumbe, 130
Zarabanda, 130
vessels, 78–80
Pantheon, 9
Parsley, poison, 32–33
Partera, 116, 135
Pataki, 9, 43, 52, 56, 135
Pentacle, 21
Pentagram, 129
Photograph, 27
Piedra Iman, 121, 135
Pigeon grass, 33
Poison hemlock, 32–33
Poison parsley, 32–33
Poleo, 120
Poppets, 36
Poteau-Mitan, 135
Prayer, 8
Prenda, 81, 135
Psychic attacks, 37

R

Rama, 49, 71, 135
Rayado, 82, 136
Recetas, 136
Red Sanders, 32
Regla de Ocha. *See* Santeria
Religious culture
anthropological terms, 9
common elements, 7–8
magic in (*See* Magico-religious culture(s))
Religious experience, 8
Resguardo, 85, 136
Responder issues
behavior, 125
communication, 125–126
Curanderismo, 122–123
generalizations, avoidance of, 126
harmful implements, 39
language, 125
in Palo Mayombe, 86–87
patience, 125
patient behavior, 125
responsibility when finding Nganga, 86
in Santeria, 67–68
in Voodooism, 107–108
weapons, 39
in Wiccan religion, 38–39
Ritual(s), 8, 9
area preparation, 22
tools, 20–21
consecration of, 22
Wiccan religion, 20–21
Ritual body art, 36
Rompe Saraguey, 65

S

Sabbat, 25, 136
Sacred object and place, 8
Sage, 34, 38, 120
Sahumerio, 118, 136
Salt, 27
San Martin Caballero, 111, 112
San Martin de Porres, 111
San Simon, 113
San Toribio Romo, 113
Sandalwood, 32
Sangre Debil, 118
Santa Marta, 113
Santeria, 41–69
  ancestor reverence, 48–49
  animal sacrifices, 57–58
  articles of comfort, 66
  belief and practices, 43–49
  Brujeria, 60
  deities, 43–48 (*See also specific gods*)
    Aganyu, 47–48, 63
    Aggayu, 58
    Babalu-Aye, 46
    Chango, 45
    Elegua, 43–44
    Ibeji, 47, 61
    Inle, 48
    Obatala, 45
    Ochosi, 45, 57, 61
    Ogun, 45
    Oko, 48
    Olokun, 46, 63
    Osain, 47, 63, 64
    Oshun, 45, 47
    Oya, 45–46
    Yemaya, 46, 47
  Ebbo, 57–58, 133
  espiritismo, 59–60
  group structure, 49–50
  healing and sickness, 62–65
    head cleansing, 63
    methods, 63–65
  herbalism, 64–65
  High Priest, 42, 47, 50, 131
  history, 41–43
  holy days, 61–62
  Itutu, 62
  necklaces, 50–52
    common versions of, 51
  offerings and sacrifices, 56–57
  responder issues, 67–68
  rituals and ceremonies, 50–57
    cofa, 52
    Diloggun, 56
    Kariocha, 53–54
    mercury in, 66
    Obi, 54–56
    Patakis, 56
    receiving necklaces, 50–52
    warrior, 52
  sacred spaces, 62
  trance possession, 58–59
Scapulario, 121
Scented mayweed, 33
Scourge, 21
Seven Congos, 80
Shamanism, 14
Siam weed, 65
Siete Rayos, 74
  sacred vessel, 78, 80
Significance of human life, 7
Simbi, 93, 94, 101
Skyclad, 39, 136
Smudging, 34
Sobo, 92
Sobrador, 115, 136
Solar Cross, 128
Spearmint, 65, 120
Sporobolus, 65
St. John's plant, 33
St. Joseph's wort, 33
Statues, 27
Stinging nettle, 33
Stones, 37
Stregheria, 17
Susto, 2, 117, 120, 136
Sweat lodges, 36
Sweet Basil, 120
Swords, 98
Symbols, 9, 127–130

T

Taboo(s), 9, 37–38
Tambor, 61, 136
Tata Nfumbe, 74, 130
Te De Nurranjo, 120
The Ibejis, 47
Theurgy, 10
Thor's Hammer, 128
Thyme, 32

Ti-Bon Ange, 95, 105, 106, 136
Ti-Bon Anj, 95, 105, 136
Ti-Jean Petro, 94
Tiembla Tierra, 74
  sacred vessel, 79
Trance possession, 10
Triple Goddess, 129
Tyre Rune, 127

V

Valknot, 127
Vervain, 33
Voodon, 136
Voodoo, 89–108
  altar, 103, 104
  artifacts, 104
  beliefs and practices, 89–98
  ceremonies, 99–102
    entrance, 100–101
    initiation, 102
    Manje Loa, 100–101
    marriage, 102
    Priye Ginen, 100–101
    rites of passage, 101
    spirit possession, 101–102
  deities, 90–95
    Agassou, 92
    Agwe, 93, 101, 104, 128
    Ayido Wedo, 92
    Ayizan, 91
    Azaka, 92, 101, 104
    Baron Loa, 104
    Baron Samedi, 94
    Carrefour, 93
    Damballah Wedo, 92, 128
    Ezili Danto, 94, 101, 104
    Ezili Freda, 92, 104
    Ezulie Dantor, 94, 128
    food offerings, 101
    Gede, 94, 101, 104
    Gran Bwa, 93, 129
    Kalfu, 93
    La Sirene, 92, 104
    Legba, 90, 101, 104, 128
    Loko, 91
    Maman Brigette, 95
    Marasa, 90
    Marinette-Bwa-Chech, 94
    Ogou group, 93, 101, 104, 128
    Simbi, 93, 94
    Sobo, 92
    Ti-Jean Petro, 94
  Dominican, 106
  drums, 98–99
    Congo, 98
    Petro, 98
    Rada, 98
  entrance, 100–101
  group structure, 95–96
  health and sickness, 105–106
  initiation, 102
  Manje Loa, 100–101
  marriage, 102
  New Orleans, 106–107
  responder issues, 107–108
  rites of passage, 101
  ritual tools, 96–99
    Asson, 96–97
    bottles, 97
    chromolithograph, 97
    conch shell, 98
    drums, 98–99
    flags, 97
    Govi, 97
    Ogan, 98
    packets, 98
    swords, 98
    triangles, 98
    zins, 98
  sacred days, 102–103
  sacred spaces, 103–104
    altar, 103, 104
    temple, 103
  spirit possession, 101–102
  spiritual bodies and guardians, 95
  symbols, 128–129
  temple, 103
  West African, 106
  zombies, 102

W

Wand, 21
Wanga, 98, 136
Watchtower, 23, 136
Weapons, 39
West African Voodoo, 106
Wheel of the Year, 129
White star, 33
Wiccan religion, 13, 14
  Alexandrian, 16, 19

altar, 26
articles of comfort, 36–37
  amulets, 36
  jewelry, 36–37
  stones, 37
beliefs, 17–18
British Traditional, 16
cakes and wines, 24
calling the quarters, 23
candles, 34–35
Celtic, 16
ceremonies, 21
circle
  banishment of, 24
  casting the, 22–23
correspondences, 21–22
deities, 15, 18
  aspects, 131
  female, 15
destruction of illness, 35–36
  poppets, 36
  ritual body art, 36
  sweat lodges, 36
Dianic, 16
Eclectic, 16
energy raising, 24
ethics, 18–19
first responder issues, 38–39
Gardenarian, 16–17
Georgian, 17
grounding, 22
group structure, 19–20
healing techniques, 29–33
  absent, 31
  aromatherapy, 29
  auric, 29–30
  chakras, 31
  chanting, 29
  cord healing, 29
  herbalism, 31–33
Hereditary, 17
history, 15–16
holy days, 25–26
  Beltane, 26
  Imbolc, 25
  Lammas, 26
  Litha, 26
  Mabon, 26
  Ostara, 26
  Samhain, 25
  Yule, 25
illness, 35–36
invocation of deity, 23
Mohsian tradition, 17
rites of passage, 24–25
  coming of age, 24
  funeral, 25
  handfasting, 24–25
  wiccaning, 24
ritual body art, 33
rituals, 21
  tools, 20–21
sacred places, 26–29
  objects at, 27–28
smudging, 34
sources of sickness, 37
  cursed objects, 37
  psychic attacks, 37
spellwork, 24
Strega tradition, 17
symbols, 129
  Horned God, 129
  Labrys, 129
  Lambrynth, 129
  Pentagram, 129
  Triple Goddess, 129
  Wheel of the Year, 129
taboos, 37–38
traditions, 16–17
Widdershins, 23, 24, 136
Witch hazel, 65
Witches herb, 33
Worldview, 9

Y

Yemaya, 46, 47
  animal sacrifice for, 58
  celebrations day, 61
  divine punishment, 63
  necklace, 51
  offering to, 57
Yerba Buena, 65, 120
Yerbero, 116, 136
Yunkagua, 85

Z

Zarabanda, 75, 130
  sacred vessel, 78
Zins, 98
Zombies, 102